Prayers that Rout Demons

John Eckhardt

Charisma
HOUSE
A STRANG COMPANY

Most STRANG COMMUNICATIONS BOOK GROUP products are available at special quantity discounts for bulk purchase for sales promotions, premiums, fund-raising, and educational needs. For details, write Strang Communications Book Group, 600 Rinehart Road, Lake Mary, Florida 32746, or telephone (407) 333-0600.

PRAYERS THAT ROUT DEMONS by John Eckhardt
Published by Charisma House
A Strang Company
600 Rinehart Road
Lake Mary, Florida 32746
www.strangbookgroup.com

Unless otherwise noted, all Scripture quotations are from the King James Version of the Bible.

Design Director: Bill Johnson
Cover design by Jerry Pomales

This publication is translated in Spanish under the title *Oraciones que derrotan a los demonios*, copyright © 2009 by John Eckhardt, published by Casa Creación, a Strang company. All rights reserved.

Library of Congress Cataloging-in-Publication Data
Eckhardt, John, 1957-
  Prayers that rout demons / John Eckhardt.
     p. cm.
  ISBN 978-1-59979-246-0
  1. Spiritual warfare. 2. Prayers. I. Title.
  BS680.S73E25 2008
  242'.8--dc22
                                    2007036947

09 10 11 12 13 — 13 12 11 10 9 8
Printed in the United States of America

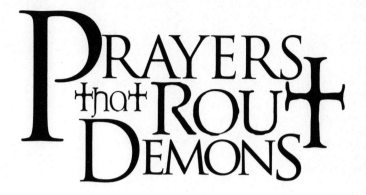

CONTENTS

III—Confronting the Enemy's Tactics

IV—Destroying the Enemy's Forces

V—EXPERIENCING DELIVERANCE AND RELEASE

FOREWORD

IRST, I WOULD LIKE TO THANK OUR LORD AND SAVIOR Jesus Christ for giving Apostle John Eckhardt such boldness and love for His people. During the years that I have known Apostle Eckhardt, I have found him to be a man who loves God and God's people. He has been found to be faithful to the Lord, his family, and the ministry. I have observed him increase in the revelation of God's Word and knowledge of deliverance. Apostle Eckhardt has never compromised or been afraid to preach the truth, whereas other pastors would not address these issues because of losing members and/or money. His concern is getting God's people free.

I have had many people throughout the years tell me that Apostle Eckhardt has helped them in many areas of their lives. There are many testimonies throughout the United States and all over the world of people being delivered through his ministry. He has written several books and recorded several tapes and CDs that have assisted people in getting free from things that seemed hopeless. Personally, I can say that Apostle Eckhardt's ministry has been a blessing to me.

Apostle Eckhardt has a special anointing and the wisdom to put such awesome and powerful warfare prayers together to enlighten and equip the body of Christ. This book is powerful on impact and is guaranteed to help in every area of your life. Often times people are bound by witchcraft and curses but do not know how to be free. Whereas most Christians are unaware of curses that affect their lives, Apostle Eckhardt's book reveals curses and how to break the curses and bind the enemy. This book gives you the prayers that break every demonic stronghold on your life. Upon reading these prayers, the power of God will set you free from witchcraft, curses, and idolatry, and healing will be loosed in your life. This book deals with remedies for overthrowing the powers of darkness and principalities and for breaking curses on your land. The same prayers could be used for your city. Also, these prayers will get the dark areas out of your life so that God can use you in greater ways. After breaking the curse, Apostle Eckhardt teaches you how to loose blessings over yourself and your family. If you have ever desired the fire of God in your life, this book teaches you how to release the fire of the living God to preach, prophesy, heal the sick, and cast out devils.

This book is a must-have for every believer.

—RUTH BROWN
Author, *Destroying the Works of Witchcraft Through Fasting & Prayer*

INTRODUCTION

P*RAYERS* T*HAT* R*OUT* D*EMONS* COMBINES PRAYER AND confession of the Word of God to bring breakthrough against any demonic opposition. Prayer and confession of the Word are two of the most powerful weapons believers have. You will see a great release of God's power when these two are combined.

I began writing these prayers as I studied the Word of God. The Holy Spirit illuminated many scriptures to me that needed to be released through prayer. I began to see clearly the plan of God for believers and how the enemy wanted to stop that plan. The Lord taught me the importance of praying the Word to overcome spiritual resistance to the plan of God for my life.

These prayers have been forged over a period of many years. They have been birthed out of warfare and deliverance. They have come from years of experience in ministering to individuals and nations. The Holy Spirit has helped me understand many scriptures and how to use them in prayer.

Most of the prayers in this book will have scriptural references. We base our prayers on the Word of God. The Word of God will inspire you to pray. The promises of God will motivate you to pray. God has given us many great and precious promises. It is through faith and promises we inherit the promises (Heb. 6:12).

There are many believers who struggle with prayer. Many say they don't know how to pray. Some have become discouraged in prayer. This book will help you learn how to pray with revelation and authority. These prayers are designed to see results. We have received many testimonies of people coming to another level in their prayer lives by using these prayers. They are written to be simple, yet powerful.

There are many different kinds of prayers in this book. We are told to pray with all kinds of prayers (Eph. 6:8). These prayers will expand your ability to pray. You will pray many different kinds of prayers that you ordinarily would not have prayed. This will help to break the limitations off of your prayer life.

Prayer is one of the ways we release the will of God upon the earth. We must study the Word of God in order to know the will of God. This is why prayer and the Word must be combined. Daniel was able to pray effectively because he knew the Word of God concerning His people (Dan. 9:2–3).

We should pray with understanding (1 Cor. 14:15). Understanding the will of God will help us pray correctly. The Word of God is the will of God. We are not to be unwise, but understanding of what the will of the Lord is (Eph. 5:17). Prayer also helps us walk perfectly and completely in all the will of God (Col. 4:12).

Life and death are in the power of the tongue (Prov. 18:21). Right words are forcible (Job 6:25). The words we speak are spirit and life (John 6:63). We can be snared by the words of our mouth. We need to articulate the thoughts of God by praying and confessing His Word (Isa. 55:8). God's Word released through our tongue will cause His power to manifest in our lives.

Words are used to convey our thoughts. The words of God are the thoughts of God. We are releasing the mind of God when we pray and confess His Word. The thoughts of God are peace and prosperity (Jer. 29:11). They are designed to bring us to an expected end.

Jesus taught us that our faith is released through our words (Mark 11:23). Our faith-filled words can move mountains. There is nothing impossible to those who believe. Our faith is a key to seeing miracles and breakthrough on a consistent basis. Whatever we ask in prayer, believing, we will receive (Matt. 21:22).

The Word is near us (Rom. 10:8). The Word is in our mouth and heart. This is the Word of faith. The mouth and the heart are connected. We speak from the abundance of the heart. The Word of God in our heart will come through our mouth. Faith in the heart will be released through our mouth. God watches over His Word to perform it (Jer. 1:12).

We are encouraged to call upon the Lord. He has promised to show us great and mighty things (Jer. 33:3). The Lord delights in our prayers. He delights in answering our prayers. Before we call, He will answer (Isa. 65:24). The Lord's ears are open unto the prayers of the righteous (1 Pet. 3:12). The effectual fervent prayer of a righteous man avails much (James 5:16). We are told to pray without ceasing (1 Thess. 5:17).

Our God hears prayer. All flesh should come to Him in prayer (Ps. 65:2). This book is designed for believers in any nation. All believers have similar challenges. All believers must overcome these challenges. God is no respecter of persons. He is near to all who call upon Him (Ps. 145:19). The Lord will hear your supplication and will receive your prayer (Ps. 6:9).

Calling upon the Lord will bring salvation and deliverance from your enemies (Ps. 18:3). This has always been a key to deliverance. You can pray yourself out of any adverse situation. The Lord is your helper. God will not turn away your prayer (Ps. 66:20). God will not despise your prayer (Ps. 102:17). The prayer of the upright is God's delight (Prov. 15:8).

We have been given the keys of the kingdom (Matt. 16:19). This gives us the authority to bind and loose. To *bind* means to restrict, stop, hinder, fetter, check, hold back, arrest, or put a stop to. To *loose* means to untie, unbind, unlock, liberate, release, forgive, or free. Keys represent the authority to lock (bind) or unlock (loose). Prayer and confession are two of the ways we use this authority. We can bind the works of darkness, which include: sickness, disease, hurt, witchcraft, poverty, death, destruction, confusion, defeat, and discouragement. We can loose ourselves and others from the works of darkness. This will result in greater liberty and prosperity.

Binding and loosing will help us in the area of deliverance. We can loose ourselves from many things by using our authority. We can loose others by praying these prayers. Jesus came to destroy the works of the devil. He came that we might have life in abundance.

Believers must know and operate in authority. Jesus gave His disciples power and authority over all devils (Matt. 10:1). We are seated with Christ in heavenly places far above all principality and power (Eph. 1:20; 2:6). Believers can use this authority through prayer and confession. We have authority to tread upon serpents and scorpions (Luke 10:19). Jesus promised that nothing would hurt us. Many believers suffer unnecessarily because they fail to exercise their authority.

These prayers are for believers who have a hatred for the works of darkness (Ps. 139:21). Do you hate every false way (Ps. 119:104)? Do you want to see changes in your city, region, and nation? You are a king, and you have the power to change geographic regions (Eccles. 8:4). The fear of the Lord is to hate evil (Prov. 8:13).

The prayers in this book are designed to demolish strongholds. God's Word is like a hammer that breaks the rock in pieces (Jer. 23:29). We need powerful prayers to demolish these strongholds. These prayers are for those who want to see breakthroughs in their personal lives as well as in their cities, regions, and nations. There have been many prayer books written over the years, but I believe this prayer book is unique in its simplicity and revelation.

Satan has been defeated through the cross. Principalities and powers have been spoiled (Col. 2:15). We are enforcing this victory through our prayers. We are executing the judgments written. This honor is given to all His saints. The saints have possessed the kingdom (Dan. 7:18). This means we have authority with the King to advance the reign of Christ over the nations.

David was a king who understood the place of prayer in victory. He had many victories over his enemies. He saw mighty deliverance through prayer. He prayed for the defeat of his enemies and God answered him. We will have the same results over our spiritual enemies. We are not wrestling against flesh and blood. We must overcome principalities and powers with the armor of God. We must take the sword of the Spirit and pray with all prayer (Eph. 6:12–18).

The prayers of David ended with Psalm 72:20. He ended them by praying that the whole earth would be filled with God's glory. This is the end of prayer. We believe that the earth will be filled with the knowledge of the glory of the Lord as the waters cover the sea (Hab. 2:14). This is our goal. We will continue to pray toward the fulfillment of this promise. We will see the growth of God's kingdom and the destruction of the powers of darkness through our prayers. Revival and glory are increasing. Our prayers are like gasoline to the fire.

SECTION 1

PLUGGING into the POWER SOURCE

OUR SOURCE OF POWER IS THE HOLY SPIRIT AND THE Word OF God. We build ourselves up in faith when we confess the Word of God. We experience greater confidence when we understand the Word and walk in revelation. Prayer plugs us into the power source. Prayer connects us to God and allows His power to flow to us in any situation.

Salvation is the basis for warfare. The new birth is a necessity. A believer also needs the infilling of the Holy Spirit. Are you born again? Do you know beyond a doubt that you are saved? Believers must live holy lives that are submitted to the Holy Spirit. We are commanded to walk in the Spirit. This will assure us of continual victory and breakthroughs for others. We can revenge disobedience when our obedience is fulfilled. Jesus cast out devils through the power of the Holy Spirit (Matt. 12:28). The Holy Spirit was the source of His power and wisdom.

This section of prayers that teach us how to plug into the power source—God's Holy Spirit and God's Word—is not for religious people. These are not religious prayers that begin to work when someone recites them. These prayers are for born-again believers who desire to see the growth of the kingdom of God.

We are told to be strong in the Lord and in the power of His might (Eph. 6:10). We walk and war in His strength. This requires humility and total dependence upon God. We are not confident in our own strength. We cannot allow pride to open the door for destruction.

The Lord is a man of war (Exod. 15:3). He will fight our battles. We depend upon His power and direction. We depend upon His Word and His Spirit. I cannot overemphasize the need for humility. God gives grace to the humble.

The Lord is the strength of my life. This gives me the ability to overcome all fear. I will put my trust in Him. This was the key to David's victories. David was a king who knew how to depend upon the Lord. David won many battles and overcame all of his enemies.

The Lord taught David how to war (Ps. 144:1). He will also teach you how to war. You must depend on Him. The prayers and strategies in this book were learned from years of warring and trusting in God. God taught us how to war using His Word. The Holy Spirit opened our eyes to great truths, and we are still learning.

God was David's power source. He confessed that the Lord was his strength. David was a man of prayer and worship. He enjoyed the Lord's presence. The Lord's presence was David's source of joy and strength. His songs were powerful prophetic weapons against the enemy. There is no substitute for a life of praise and worship. Every believer needs to belong to a church that is strong in praise and worship.

There are many great warriors being trained in the school of the Holy Spirit. They are humble people who had to depend upon God for breakthrough. They had to connect with the Lord, who is the greatest warrior. They learned through experience and sometimes through failure. Like these great warriors for God, if we call upon the Lord, He will show us great and mighty things.

The Word of God is the sword of the Spirit. A sword is used

in war. The Lord will teach you how to use this sword. You will use it against the spiritual enemies of your soul. You will see great victories as you use it correctly. Most of the prayers in this book have a scriptural reference. I would encourage you to look at the verses and meditate on them. The Word of God is our source of wisdom. We operate in God's wisdom to defeat the powers of hell.

Confessing the Word of God is an important part of every believer's spiritual life. Christianity is called *the great confession*. Salvation comes from confessing with the mouth. The mouth is connected to the heart. The Word of God released from your mouth will be planted in your heart. Faith is released from the mouth. The mouth can only release what is in the heart. Faith in the heart that is released through the mouth can move mountains.

God is the source of all our victories and breakthrough. He is the source of our wisdom and strategies. His Word is the source for our understanding of the warfare in which we are involved. Our warfare originates in the heavens. We bind what is already bound in the heavens. We loose what is already loosed in the heavens.

God has illuminated many scriptures to us over the years of being involved in deliverance and warfare. These scriptures have been invaluable in helping us experience breakthrough. The Word of God is a treasure chest of wisdom and knowledge. It contains an abundance of revelation for every believer. Every believer who desires to enjoy liberty and victory must take time to study the Word of God and ask for revelation.

One of my favorite group of prayers in this section are those called "Prayers for Revelation." When I began to pray these prayers, the results were dramatic. I began to see truths in the Word of God that I had never seen. Revelation is the key to authority. Peter received the keys of the kingdom after he received the revelation that Jesus was Christ (Matt. 16:16).

God has promised to make us joyful in the house of prayer (Isa. 56:7). God's house is called a *house of prayer* for all nations. I believe we should not only pray but also enjoy prayer. The joy of the Lord is our strength. Prayer should yield an abundance of miracles and rewards. Those who enjoy the results of prayer will enjoy an exciting life.

CONFESSIONS

No weapon formed against me shall prosper, and every tongue that rises against me in judgment I condemn (Isa. 54:17).

I am established in righteousness, and oppression is far from me (Isa. 54:14).

The weapons of my warfare are not carnal but mighty through God to the pulling down of strongholds (2 Cor. 10:4).

I take the shield of faith, and I quench every fiery dart of the enemy (Eph. 6:16).

I take the sword of the Spirit, which is the Word of God, and use it against the enemy (Eph. 6:17).

I am redeemed from the curse of the law. I am redeemed from poverty. I am redeemed from sickness. I am redeemed from spiritual death (Gal. 3:13).

I overcome all because greater is He that is in me than he that is in the world (1 John 4:4).

I stand in the evil day having my loins girded about with truth, and I have the breastplate of righteousness. My feet are shod with the gospel of peace. I take the shield of faith. I am covered with the helmet of salvation, and I use the sword of the Spirit, which is the Word of God (Eph. 6:14–17).

I am delivered from the power of darkness and translated into the kingdom of God's dear Son (Col. 1:13).

I tread upon serpents and scorpions and over all the power of the enemy, and nothing shall hurt me (Luke 10:19).

I do not have the spirit of fear but power, love, and a sound mind (2 Tim. 1:7).

I am blessed with all spiritual blessings in heavenly places in Christ Jesus (Eph. 1:3).

I am healed by the stripes of Jesus (Isa. 53:5).

My hand is upon the neck of my enemies (Gen. 49:8).

You anoint my head with oil; my cup runs over. Goodness and mercy shall follow me all the days of my life (Ps. 23:5–6).

I am anointed to preach, to teach, to heal, and to cast out devils.

I receive abundance of grace and the gift of righteousness, and I reign in life through Christ Jesus (Rom. 5:17).

I have life and that more abundantly (John 10:10).

I walk in the light as He is in the light, and the blood of Jesus cleanses me from all sin (1 John 1:7).

I am the righteousness of God in Christ (2 Cor. 5:21).

I am the head and not the tail (Deut. 28:13).

I shall decree a thing, and it shall be established in my life (Job 22:28).

I have favor with God and with man (Luke 2:52).

Wealth and riches are in my house, and my righteousness endures forever (Ps. 112:3).

I will be satisfied with long life, and God will show me His salvation (Ps. 91:16).

I dwell in the secret place of the Most High, and I abide under the shadow of the Almighty (Ps. 91:1).

No evil will befall me, and no plague shall come near my dwelling (Ps. 91:10).

My children are taught of the Lord, and great is their peace (Isa. 54:13).

I am strengthened with might by His Spirit in the inner man (Eph. 3:16).

I am rooted and grounded in love (Eph. 3:17).

I bless my natural enemies, and I overcome evil with good (Matt. 5:44).

PRAYERS FOR BLESSING AND FAVOR

Lord, bless me and keep me. Make Your face to shine upon me, and be gracious unto me. Lord, lift up Your countenance upon me and give me peace (Num. 6:24–26).

Make me as Ephraim and Manasseh (Gen. 48:20).

Let me be satisfied with favor and filled with Your blessing (Deut. 33:23).

Lord, command Your blessing upon my life.

Give me revelation, and let me be blessed (Matt. 16:17).

I am the seed of Abraham through Jesus Christ, and I receive the blessing of Abraham. Lord, in blessing, bless me, and in multiplying, multiply me as the stars of heaven and as the sand of the seashore.

Let Your showers of blessing be upon my life (Ezek. 34:26).

Turn every curse sent my way into a blessing (Neh. 13:2).

Let Your blessing make me rich (Prov. 10:22).

Let all nations call me blessed (Mal. 3:12).

Let all generations call me blessed (Luke 1:48).

I am a son of the blessed (Mark 14:61).

I live in the kingdom of the blessed (Mark 11:10).

My sins are forgiven, and I am blessed (Rom. 4:7).

Lord, You daily load me with benefits (Ps. 68:19).

I am chosen by God, and I am blessed (Ps. 65:4).

My seed is blessed (Ps. 37:26).

Let me inherit the land (Ps. 37:22).

I am a part of a holy nation, and I am blessed (Ps. 33:12).

Lord, bless my latter end more than my beginning (Job 42:12).

Lord, let Your presence bless my life (2 Sam. 6:11).

I drink the cup of blessing (1 Cor. 10:16).

Lord, bless me, and cause Your face to shine upon me, that Your way may be known upon the earth and Your saving health among all nations. Let my land yield increase, and let the ends of the earth fear You (Ps. 67).

I know You favor me because my enemies do not triumph over me (Ps. 41:11).

Lord, be favorable unto my land (Ps. 85:1).

Lord, grant me life and favor (Job 10:12).

In Your favor, Lord, make my mountain stand strong (Ps. 30:7).

Lord, I entreat Your favor (Ps. 45:12).

Let Your favor cause my horn to be exalted (Ps. 89:17).

Lord, this is my set time for favor (Ps. 102:13).

Remember me, O Lord, with the favor that You bring unto Your children, and visit me with Your salvation (Ps. 106:4).

Lord, I entreat Your favor with my whole heart (Ps. 119:58).

Let Your favor be upon my life as a cloud of the latter rain (Prov. 16:15).

Let Your beauty be upon my life, and let me be well favored (Gen. 29:17).

I am highly favored (Luke 1:28).

Lord, let me receive extraordinary favor.

Prayers for Revelation

You are a God that reveals secrets. Lord, reveal Your secrets unto me (Dan. 2:28).

Reveal to me the secret and deep things (Dan. 2:22).

Let me understand things kept secret from the foundation of the world (Matt. 13:35).

Let the seals be broken from Your Word (Dan. 12:9).

Let me understand and have revelation of
Your will and purpose for my life.

Give me the spirit of wisdom and revelation, and let the
eyes of my understanding be enlightened (Eph. 1:17).

Let me understand heavenly things (John 3:12).

Open my eyes to behold wondrous things
out of Your Word (Ps. 119:18).

Let me know and understand the mysteries
of the kingdom (Mark 4:11).

Let me speak to others by revelation (1 Cor. 14:6).

Reveal Your secrets to Your servants the prophets (Amos 3:7).

Let the hidden things be made manifest (Mark 4:22).

Hide Your truths from the wise and prudent,
and reveal them to babes (Matt. 11:25).

Let Your arm be revealed in my life (John 12:38).

Reveal the things that belong to me (Deut. 29:29).

Let Your Word be revealed unto me (1 Sam. 3:7).

Let Your glory be revealed in my life (Isa. 40:5).

Let Your righteousness be revealed in my life (Isa. 56:1).

Let me receive visions and revelations of the Lord (2 Cor. 12:1).

Let me receive an abundance of revelations (2 Cor. 12:7).

Let me be a good steward of Your revelations (1 Cor. 4:1).

Let me speak the mystery of Christ (Col. 4:3).

Let me receive and understand Your hidden wisdom (1 Cor. 2:7).

Hide not Your commandments from me (Ps. 119:19).

Let me speak the wisdom of God in a mystery (1 Cor. 2:7).

Let me make known the mystery of the gospel (Eph. 6:19).

Make known unto me the mystery of Your will (Eph. 1:9).

Open Your dark sayings upon the harp (Ps. 49:4).

Let me understand Your parables; the words of
the wise and their dark sayings (Prov. 1:6).

Lord, lighten my candle and enlighten my darkness (Ps. 18:28).

Make darkness light before me (Isa. 42:16).

Give me the treasures of darkness and hidden
riches in secret places (Isa. 45:3).

Let Your candle shine upon my head (Job 29:3).

My spirit is the candle of the Lord, searching all
the inward parts of the belly (Prov. 20:27).

Let me understand the deep things of God (1 Cor. 2:10).

Let me understand Your deep thoughts (Ps. 92:5).

Let my eyes be enlightened with Your Word (Ps. 19:8).

My eyes are blessed to see (Luke 10:23).

Let all spiritual cataracts and scales be
removed from my eyes (Acts 9:18).

Let me comprehend with all saints what is the breadth and
length and depth and height of Your love (Eph. 3:18).

Let my reins instruct me in the night season, and
let me awaken with revelation (Ps. 16:7).

PRAYERS CONCERNING THE HEAVENS

I am sitting in heavenly places in Christ, far above all
principality, power, might, and dominion (Eph. 1:3).

I take my position in the heavens and bind the principalities
and powers that operate against my life in the name of Jesus.

I break and rebuke every program in the heavens
that would operate against me through the sun,
the moon, the stars, and the constellations.

I bind and rebuke any ungodly forces operating against me
through Arcturus, Pleiades, Mazzaroth, and Orion (Job 38:31–32).

I bind and rebuke all moon deities and demons operating
through the moon in the name of Jesus (2 Kings 23:5).

I bind all sun deities and demons operating through
the sun in the name of Jesus (2 Kings 23:5).

I bind all deities and demons operating through the stars
and planets in the name of Jesus (2 Kings 23:5).

The sun shall not smite me by day nor the moon by night (Ps. 121:6).

The heavens were created to be a blessing to my life.

I receive the rain and blessing from heaven
upon my life in the name of Jesus.

I pray for angels to be released to war against any spirit in the heavens
assigned to block my prayers from being answered (Dan. 10:12–13).

I bind the prince of the power of the air
in the name of Jesus (Eph. 2:2).

I pray for the floodgates of heaven to be
opened over my life (Mal. 3:10).

I pray for an open heaven, and I bind any demonic
interference from the heavens in the name of Jesus.

Let the evil powers of heaven be shaken in
the name of Jesus (Matt. 24:29).

Let the heavens drop dew upon my life (Deut. 33:28).

Bow the heavens and come down, O Lord (Ps. 144:5).

Let the heavens be opened over my life,
and let me see visions (Ezek. 1:1).

Shake the heavens and fill my house with Your glory (Hag. 2:6–7).

Thunder in the heavens against the enemy, O Lord (Ps. 18:13).

Let the heavens drop at the presence of God (Ps. 68:8).

Let the heavens praise Thy wonders, O Lord (Ps. 89:5).

Show Your wonders in the heavens (Joel 2:30).

Ride upon the heavens and release Your voice, O Lord (Ps. 68:33).

Release Your manifold wisdom to the
powers in the heavens (Eph. 3:10).

PRAYERS FOR ENLARGEMENT AND INCREASE

Break off of my life any limitations and restrictions placed
on my life by any evil spirits in the name of Jesus.

I bind and cast out all python and constrictor
spirits in the name of Jesus.

Bless me indeed, and enlarge my coast. Let Your hand
be with me, and keep me from evil (1 Chron. 4:10).

Cast out my enemies, and enlarge my borders (Exod. 34:24).

Lord, You have promised to enlarge my borders (Deut. 12:20).

Enlarge my heart so I can run the way of
Your commandments (Ps. 119:32).

My mouth is enlarged over my enemies (1 Sam. 2:1).

Enlarge my steps so I can receive Your
wealth and prosperity (Isa. 60:5–9).

I receive deliverance and enlargement for my life (Esther 4:14).

The Lord shall increase me more and more,
me and my children (Ps. 115:14).

Let Your kingdom and government increase in my life (Isa. 9:7).

Let me increase in the knowledge of God (Col. 2:19).

O Lord, bless me and increase me (Isa. 51:2).

Let me increase exceedingly (Gen. 30:43).

Let me increase with the increase of God (Col. 2:19).

Let me increase and abound in love (1 Thess. 3:12).

Increase my greatness, and comfort me on every side (Ps. 71:21).

Let me increase in wisdom and stature (Luke 2:52).

Let me increase in strength and confound the adversaries (Acts 9:22).

Let Your grace and favor increase in my life.

Let the years of my life be increased (Prov. 9:11).

Let the Word of God increase in my life (Acts 6:7).

Bless me in all my increase (Deut. 14:22).

Let my giving and tithes increase (Deut. 14:22).

Let my latter end greatly increase (Job 8:7).

Let me grow in grace and in the knowledge
of Jesus Christ (2 Pet. 3:18).

I will flourish like a palm tree and grow like
a cedar in Lebanon (Ps. 92:12).

Let my faith grow exceedingly (2 Thess. 1:3).

The breaker is gone up before me and broken through
every limitation and barrier of the enemy (Mic. 2:13).

Lord, You are the God of the breakthrough. You have
broken forth against my enemies (2 Sam. 5:20).

My branches run over every wall erected by the enemy (Gen. 49:22).

I can run through a troop and leap over a wall (Ps. 18:29).

Let my line go through all the earth, and my
words to the end of the world (Ps. 19:4).

I am a joint heir with Jesus Christ. Give me the heathen for my inheritance and the uttermost part of the earth for my possession (Ps. 2:8).

Renunciations

I renounce all lust, perversion, immorality, uncleanness, impurity, and sexual sin in the name of Jesus.

I renounce all witchcraft, sorcery, divination, and occult involvement in the name of Jesus.

I renounce all ungodly soul ties and immoral relationships in the name of Jesus.

I renounce all hatred, anger, resentment, revenge, retaliation, unforgiveness, and bitterness in the name of Jesus.

I forgive any person who has ever hurt me, disappointed me, abandoned me, mistreated me, or rejected me in the name of Jesus.

I renounce all addiction to drugs, alcohol, or any legal or illegal substance that has bound me in the name of Jesus.

I renounce all pride, haughtiness, arrogance, vanity, ego, disobedience, and rebellion in the name of Jesus.

I renounce all envy, jealousy, and covetousness in the name of Jesus.

I renounce all fear, unbelief, and doubt in the name of Jesus.

I renounce all selfishness, self-will, self-pity, self-rejection, self-hatred, and self-promotion in the name of Jesus.

I renounce all ungodly thought patterns and belief systems in the name of Jesus.

I renounce all ungodly covenants, oaths, and vows made by myself or my ancestors in the name of Jesus.

PRAYERS IN CHRIST

I am called in Christ (Rom. 1:6).

I have redemption in Christ (Rom. 3:24).

I reign in life by Christ (Rom. 5:17).

I am alive unto God through Christ (Rom. 6:11).

I have eternal life through Christ (Rom. 6:23).

I am a joint heir with Christ (Rom. 8:17).

I am sanctified in Christ (1 Cor. 1:2).

My body is a member of Christ (1 Cor. 6:15).

I have victory through Christ (1 Cor. 15:57).

I triumph in Christ (2 Cor. 2:14).

I am a new creature in Christ (2 Cor. 5:17).

I am the righteousness of God in Christ (2 Cor. 5:21).

I have liberty in Christ (Gal. 2:4).

I am crucified with Christ (Gal. 2:20).

I have put on Christ (Gal. 3:27).

I am an heir of God through Christ (Gal. 4:7).

I have been blessed with spiritual blessings in
heavenly places in Christ (Eph. 1:3).

I have been chosen in Christ before the foundation of the world,
that I should be holy and without blame before Him (Eph. 1:4).

I have obtained an inheritance in Christ (Eph. 1:11).

I have been quickened with Christ (Eph. 2:5).

I am sitting in heavenly places in Christ (Eph. 2:6).

I have been created in Christ unto good works (Eph. 2:10).

I have boldness and access in Christ (Eph. 3:12).

I rejoice in Christ (Phil. 3:3).

I press toward the mark of the high calling
of God in Christ (Phil. 3:14).

I can do all things through Christ who strengthens me (Phil. 4:13).

God supplies all my needs through Christ (Phil. 4:19).

Christ in me is the hope of glory (Col. 1:27).

I am complete in Christ (Col. 2:10).

I am dead with Christ (Col. 2:20).

I am risen with Christ (Col. 3:1).

My life is hidden with Christ in God (Col. 3:3).

Christ is my life (Col. 3:4).

I have the mind of Christ (1 Cor. 2:16).

I am a partaker of Christ (Heb. 3:14).

I am preserved in Christ (Jude 1:1).

KINGDOM PRAYERS AND DECREES

Your kingdom come; Your will be done (Matt. 6:10).

Let Your kingdom advance and be established through
preaching, teaching, and healing (Matt. 4:23).

Let the gates of my life and city be opened for
the King of glory to come in (Ps. 24:7).

Lord, You reign. You are clothed with majesty and strength. Your
throne is established of old. You are from everlasting (Ps. 93:1–2).

Lord, You are a great king above all gods (Ps. 95:3).

Let the heathen hear that the Lord reigns (Ps. 96:10).

Lord, You reign. Let the people tremble;
let the earth be moved (Ps. 99:1).

Lord, You have prepared Your throne in the heavens, and Your kingdom rules over all (Ps. 103:19).

Let men bless the Lord in all places of His dominion (Ps. 103:22).

Your kingdom is an everlasting kingdom, and Your dominion endures throughout all generations (Ps. 145:13).

Let men speak of the glory of Your kingdom and talk of Your power (Ps. 145:11).

Let men know Your mighty acts and the glorious majesty of Your kingdom (Ps. 145:12).

Let your kingdom come through deliverance (Matt. 12:22).

Let the gospel of the kingdom be preached in my region with signs and wonders following.

Father, I receive the kingdom because it is Your good pleasure to give it to me (Luke 12:32).

Let the righteousness, peace, and joy of the kingdom be established in my life (Rom. 14:17).

Let the kingdoms of this world become the kingdoms of our Lord and of His Christ (Rev. 11:15).

Let the saints possess the kingdom (Dan. 7:22).

Overthrow the thrones of wicked kingdoms (Hag. 2:22).

Preserve me unto Your heavenly kingdom (2 Tim. 4:18).

Let the scepter of Your kingdom be released (Heb. 1:8).

I seek first the kingdom of God and His righteousness, and all things are added unto me (Matt. 6:33).

Break in pieces and consume every demonic kingdom that resists your dominion (Ps. 72:8).

Let all dominions serve and obey You, O Lord (Dan. 7:27).

PRAYERS RELEASING THE FIRE OF GOD

Your throne, O Lord, is like a fiery flame (Dan. 7:9).

You are the God that answers by fire (1 Kings 18:24).

A fire goes before You, O Lord, and burns up Your enemies (Ps. 97:3).

Lord, release Your fire and burn up the works of darkness.

Baptize me with the Holy Ghost and fire (Luke 3:16).

Let Your fire be in my hands to heal the sick and cast out devils.

Let Your fire burn in my eyes, my heart,
my belly, my mouth, and my feet.

Let Your fire be in my tongue to preach and prophesy.

I receive tongues of fire.

Let Your Word be preached with fire (Jer. 23:29).

Make me a minister of fire (Heb. 1:7).

Deliver me with Your fire (Ps. 18:13).

Let Your fire protect me and cover me (Exod. 14:24).

I release the fire of God to burn up the idols of the land (Deut. 7:5).

Let the works of witchcraft and occultism
be burned in Your fire (Acts 19:19).

Purify my life with Your fire (Mal. 3:2).

Let Your fire be released in Zion (Isa. 31:9).

Let the spirits of lust and perversion be
destroyed with Your fire (Gen. 19:24).

Release the spirit of burning to burn up the
works of darkness (Ps. 140:10).

Let Your flame burn up wicked spirits (Ps. 106:18).

Let Your glory kindle a burning like the burning of a fire (Isa. 10:16).

Cause Your glorious voice to be heard. Show lightning down Your arm with a flame of devouring fire, with scattering, tempest, and hailstones (Isa. 30:30).

Let Babylon be as stubble, and let Your fire burn them. Let them not be able to deliver themselves from the power of the flame (Isa. 47:14).

Lord, come and rebuke Your enemies with flames of fire (Isa. 66:15).

Let all flesh see Your fire released (Ezek. 20:48).

Create upon Zion a flaming fire by night (Isa. 4:5).

Let the fire of Your presence be released in my life (Ps. 97:5).

Let demons be exposed and cast out with Your fire (Acts 28:3).

Release Your hot thunderbolts against the enemy (Ps. 78:48).

Cast forth lightning, and scatter the enemy (Ps. 144:6).

Let Your light be for a fire, and Your Holy One for a flame to burn the briers and thorns in my life (Isa. 10:17).

PRAYERS TO COMMAND THE MORNING, THE DAY, AND THE NIGHT

I command the morning to take hold of the ends of the earth and shake the wicked out of it (Job 38:12).

I will have dominion over the devil in the morning (Ps. 49:14).

Lord, make the outgoings of the morning to rejoice (Ps. 65:8).

I receive Your lovingkindness every morning (Ps. 143:8).

Release the beauty of Your holiness from the womb of the morning (Ps. 110:3).

Let Your light break forth in my life as the morning (Ps. 58:8).

Let Your judgments come upon the enemy morning by morning (Isa. 28:19).

Lord, Your going forth is prepared as the morning, and we pray that You will come as the rain, the latter and former rain upon the earth (Hos. 6:3).

Lord, You visit me every morning (Job 7:18).

Lord, You awaken me morning by morning. You waken my ear to hear as the learned (Isa. 50:4).

I will not be afraid of the arrow that flies by day or the terror that comes at night (Ps. 91:5).

Lord, show forth Your salvation in my life from day to day (Ps. 96:2).

I bind the screech owl in the name of Jesus (Isa. 34:14).

I bind any attack upon my life at night.

I take authority over every demon that is released against me and my family at night.

Let the evening tide trouble the enemies that would attack my life in the name of Jesus (Isa. 17:12–14).

I bind and rebuke every spirit that would creep against me at night (Ps. 104:20).

I bind and rebuke the pestilence that walks in darkness (Ps. 91:6).

I will rest at night because the Lord gives me sleep.

Let Your angels guard and protect me at night.

Lord, give me deliverance in the night season (Acts 12:6–7).

Lord, let my reins instruct me in the night season (Ps. 16:7).

Your song shall be with me in the night (Ps. 42:8).

I will meditate upon You in the night watches (Ps. 63:6).

I receive Your knowledge in the night (Ps. 19:2).

I receive Your faithfulness every night (Ps. 92:2).

I bind and rebuke every vampire spirit in the name of Jesus (Lev. 11:19).

I bind and rebuke all incubus and succubus spirits that would attack at night in the name of Jesus.

I bind and take authority over all nightmares and demonic dreams at night in the name of Jesus.

I am set in my ward whole nights (Isa. 21:8).

RELEASING THE SWORD OF THE LORD

I release the sword of the Lord against the powers of hell in the name of Jesus (Judg. 7:18).

I will whet my glittering sword and render Your vengeance against the enemy (Deut. 32:41).

Gird Your sword upon Your thigh, and ride prosperously through the earth (Ps. 45:3).

Let your enemies fall by the sword (Ps. 63:10).

Let the Assyrian fall with the sword (Isa. 31:8).

I release the sword of the Lord against leviathan (Isa. 27:1).

Send Your angels with flaming swords to fight my battles in the heavens.

I release the two-edged sword to execute judgments written (Ps. 149:6).

Release the sword out of Your mouth against the enemy (Rev. 19:15).

RELEASING THE ARROWS OF THE LORD

I release the arrow of the Lord's deliverance in my life (2 Kings 13:17).

I release Your sharp arrows into the heart of the King's enemies (Ps. 45:5).

Ordain and release Your arrows against my persecutors (Ps. 7:13).

Send out Your arrows, and scatter the enemy (Ps. 18:14).

Make my enemies turn their back with Your
arrows upon Your strings (Ps. 21:12).

Shoot out Your arrows, and destroy them (Ps. 144:6).

Send Your arrows abroad (Ps. 77:17).

Send out arrows of light into the kingdom of darkness (Hab. 3:11).

Heap mischief upon them, and spend Your
arrows upon them (Deut. 32:23).

Shoot Your arrows upon them, and let them
be wounded suddenly (Ps. 64:7).

Let Your arrow go forth as lightning against the enemy (Zech. 9:14).

Break their bones, and pierce them through
with Your arrows (Num. 24:8).

Shoot at Your enemies with Your arrows (Ps. 64:7).

Set Your mark upon my enemies for Your arrows (Lam. 3:12).

Make Your arrows bright, and release Your
vengeance upon my enemies (Jer. 51:11).

BREAKING CURSES AND CASTING OUT GENERATIONAL SPIRITS

I am redeemed from the curse of the law (Gal. 3:13).

I break all generational curses of pride, lust, perversion,
rebellion, witchcraft, idolatry, poverty, rejection, fear, confusion,
addiction, death, and destruction in the name of Jesus.

I command all generational spirits that came into my life
during conception, in the womb, in the birth canal, and
through the umbilical cord to come out in the name of Jesus.

I break all spoken curses and negative words that I
have spoken over my life in the name of Jesus.

I break all spoken curses and negative words spoken over my life by others, including those in authority in the name of Jesus.

I command all ancestral spirits of freemasonry, idolatry, witchcraft, false religion, polygamy, lust, and perversion to come out of my life in the name of Jesus.

I command all hereditary spirits of lust, rejection, fear, sickness, infirmity, disease, anger, hatred, confusion, failure, and poverty to come out of my life in the name of Jesus.

I break the legal rights of all generational spirits operating behind a curse in the name of Jesus. You have no legal right to operate in my life.

I bind and rebuke all familiar spirits and spirit guides that would try to operate in my life from my ancestors in the name of Jesus.

I renounce all false beliefs and philosophies inherited by my ancestors in the name of Jesus.

I break all curses on my finances from any ancestors that cheated or mishandled money in the name of Jesus.

I break all curses of sickness and disease and command all inherited sickness to leave my body in the name of Jesus.

Through Jesus, my family is blessed (Gen. 12:3).

I renounce all pride inherited from my ancestors in the name of Jesus.

I break all oaths, vows, and pacts made with the devil by my ancestors in the name of Jesus.

I break all curses by agents of Satan spoken against my life in secret in the name of Jesus (Ps. 10:7).

I break all written curses that would affect my life in the name of Jesus (2 Chron. 34:24).

I break every time-released curse that would activate in my life as I grow older in the name of Jesus.

I break every curse Balaam hired against my
life in the name of Jesus (Neh. 13:2).

Lord, turn every curse spoken against my
life into a blessing (Neh. 13:2).

I break all generational rebellion that would cause
me to resist the Holy Spirit (Acts 7:51).

I break all curses of death spoken by people in authority
in my nation over my nation in the name of Jesus.

I break curses of death spoken against America by
people from other nations in the name of Jesus.

Annulling Ungodly Covenants

I break and disannul all ungodly covenants, oaths, and
pledges I have made with my lips in the name of Jesus.

I renounce and break all ungodly oaths made by my
ancestors to idols, demons, false religions, or ungodly
organizations in the name of Jesus (Matt. 5:33).

I break and disannul all covenants with death and
hell made by my ancestors in the name of Jesus.

I break and disannul all ungodly covenants made with idols or
demons by my ancestors in the name of Jesus (Exod. 23:32).

I break and disannul all blood covenants made through
sacrifice that would affect my life in the name of Jesus.

I command all demons that claim any legal right to my life
through covenants to come out in the name of Jesus.

I break and disannul any covenant made with false
gods and demons through the occult involvement
and witchcraft in the name of Jesus.

I break and disannul all spirit marriages that would cause incubus
and succubus demons to attack my life in the name of Jesus.

I break and disannul any marriage to any demon
that would affect my life in the name of Jesus.

I break all agreements with hell in the name of Jesus (Isa. 28:18).

I have a covenant with God through the blood of Jesus
Christ. I am joined to the Lord, and I am one spirit
with Him. I break all ungodly covenants and renew my
covenant to God through the body and blood of Jesus.

I divorce myself from any demon that would claim my life
through any ancestral covenants in the name of Jesus.

I bind and cast out any family demon that would follow my
life through ancestral covenants in the name of Jesus.

SECTION 2

PREPARING to ENGAGE the ENEMY

WHAT MAKES A PERSON SUCCESSFUL IN SPIRITUAL warfare? Some of the qualifications include:

- *Endurance* (2 Tim. 2:3)—the ability to endure and withstand hardship, adversity, or stress. We are to endure hardness as a good soldier of Jesus Christ.

- *Hatred* (Ps. 139:22)—extreme dislike or antipathy, loathing. In spiritual warfare, we must have a hatred of evil and evil spirits.

- *Knowledge* (2 Cor. 2:11)—we are not to be ignorant of Satan's devices.

- *Persistence* (Ps. 18:37)—the ability to go on resolutely or stubbornly in spite of oppression. We must be persistent in dealing with the enemy.

- *Separation* (2 Tim. 2:14)—to get or keep apart. No man who wars entangles himself with the affairs of this life.

God uses ordinary people to accomplish His purposes. Our ability comes through grace. Every believer is sitting in heavenly places in Christ. Your position in Christ is high above all principality and power. You must see who you are *in Christ*. You can do all things through Christ.

It is important to know your authority and engage the enemy in faith. There is no need to fear. Demons are subject to the authority of the believer. Jesus gives us power to tread on serpents and scorpions (Luke 10:19). He promised that nothing will by any means harm us.

Joshua was told to engage the enemy (Deut. 2:24). You will see great victories through engagement. To *engage* means to bring troops into conflict. There are some believers who fear engagement. They are afraid of backlash. Jesus sent His disciples out to engage the enemy. They were told to heal the sick and cast out devils.

Two important revelations every believer needs are an understanding of *power* and an understanding of *authority*. *Power* is the Greek word *dunamis*. Authority is the Greek word *exousia*. Authority is the legal right to use power. We have been given authority to use the power supplied by the Holy Spirit.

Authority and power must be used. You use them by faith. This is not based on feeling but on faith. It is based on the Word of God. Faith comes by hearing the Word of God. It is important for believers to attend churches that teach on power and authority. It is important to read and study on these subjects. Revelation in these areas will give confidence to pray these prayers.

We have been given the legal right to use the name of Jesus. The name of Jesus is above every name. Authority in the name of Jesus is recognized by the spirit realm. We cast out demons in that name. We bind the works of darkness in that name. We teach and preach in that name.

We receive power through the Holy Spirit (Acts 1:8). God is able to do exceeding abundantly according to the power that operates in us. Jesus cast out demons through the power of the Holy Spirit (Matt. 12:28). We combine the power of the Holy Spirit with the authority of the name of Jesus to rout the enemy. We do not engage the enemy in our own power and authority. We engage the enemy through the power of the Holy Spirit and in the authority of the name of Jesus.

Demons recognize power and authority. They recognize believers who operate in power and authority. The more you exercise power and authority, the more you will develop in these areas. It is important to start. The prayers in this book will help you get started.

It is also important to make sure your sins are forgiven when engaging the enemy. If we confess our sins, He is faithful and just to forgive us, and to cleanse us from all unrighteousness (1 John 1:9). Do not engage the enemy with unconfessed sin in your life. There is power in the blood of Jesus. His blood cleanses us from all sin. Give no place to the devil. You must operate in righteousness.

We are made righteous through faith. We are the righteousness of God in Christ (2 Cor. 5:21). Many believers suffer from feelings of inferiority and low self-esteem because they do not understand righteousness. Righteousness gives us confidence. Righteousness gives us boldness. Righteousness is the scepter of the kingdom (Heb. 1:8). The righteous are as bold as a lion (Prov. 28:1).

God covers our heads in the day of battle (Ps. 140:7). A covering is protection. Covering is based on subjection to God, His Word, and the Holy Spirit. Humility and submission are important characteristics of believers who engage in spiritual warfare. These prayers are not for people who are rebellious. It is important to be submitted to proper biblical authority. This includes being submitted to godly leaders who watch for your soul.

PRAYERS FOR DIVINE SAFETY AND PROTECTION

I cover myself, my family, and my possessions with the blood of Jesus.

Let the fire of God surround and protect
my life from all destruction.

Let the angel of the Lord encamp around
me and protect me (Ps. 34:7).

Let Your glory be my covering and protect my back.

Hold me up, and I will be safe (Ps. 119:117).

The name of Jesus is a strong tower. I run
into it, and I am safe (Prov. 18:10).

Lord, You make me to dwell in safety (Ps. 4:8).

Set me in safety from them who puff at me (Ps. 12:5).

Let me dwell in my land safely (Lev. 26:5).

Lead me safely, and I will not fear. Let the sea
overwhelm my enemies (Ps. 78:53).

Let me lie down and rest in safety (Job 11:18; Isa. 14:30).

I will dwell in safety; nothing
shall make me afraid (Ezek. 34:28).

Keep me as the apple of Your eye, and hide me
under the shadow of Your wings (Ps. 17:8).

I will trust in the covert of Your wings (Ps. 61:4).

In the shadow of Your wings will I trust (Ps. 57:1).

Be my covert from the storm and the rain (Isa. 4:6).

Be my covert from the wind and the tempest (Isa. 32:2).

Cover my head in the day of battle (Ps. 140:7).

Cover me with the shadow of Your hand (Isa. 51:16).

Cover me with Your feathers (Ps. 91:4).

Be my defense and refuge (Ps. 59:16).

Defend and deliver me (Isa. 31:5).

Let Your glory be my defense (Isa. 4:5).

Defend me from those who rise up against me (Ps. 59:1).

Lord, You are my shield and my hiding place (Ps. 119:114).

Lord, surround me with Your shield of protection (Ps. 5:12).

Bring them down, O Lord, my shield (Ps. 59:11).

Let Your truth be my shield (Ps. 91:4).

Lord, You are my sun and shield (Ps. 84:11).

Lord, You are my shield and exceeding great reward (Gen. 15:1).

I will not be afraid of ten thousand that have set themselves against me, because You are a shield for me (Ps. 3:1–6).

You are a strong tower from the enemy (Ps. 61:3).

PRAYERS TO RELEASE THE ARM OF THE LORD

No one has an arm like You, Lord, full of power and might (Job 40:9).

Lord, You have a mighty arm. Your hand is strong, and Your right hand is high (Ps. 89:13).

Stretch out Your arm and deliver me, and rid me out of all bondage (Exod. 6:6).

Let fear and dread fall upon the enemy by the greatness of Your arm until I pass over (Exod. 15:16).

Favor me, and let Your right arm bring me into my possession (Ps. 44:3).

Break Rahab in pieces, and scatter Your enemies with Your strong arm (Ps. 89:10).

Let Your hand establish me, and let Your arm strengthen me (Ps. 89:21).

Your right hand and Your holy arm give me victory (Ps. 98:1).

Show lightning down Your arm against my enemies (Isa. 30:30).

I trust in Your arm for my salvation (Isa. 51:5).

Awake, awake, and put on strength, O arm of the Lord. Awake as in the ancient days. Cut Rahab, and wound the dragon (Isa. 51:9).

Make bare Your holy arm in the sight of all nations, and let all flesh see Your salvation (Isa. 52:10).

Show strength with Your arm, and scatter the proud (Luke 1:51).

Reveal Your arm unto me, that I might know Your strength and power.

Let the power in Your hands be released in my life (Hab. 3:4).

RELEASING THE POWER OF GOD

Lord, release Your glorious power against the enemy (Exod. 15:6).

Let power and might be released from Your hand (1 Chron. 29:12).

Scatter the enemy by Your power (Ps. 59:11).

Rule over Your enemies through Your power (Ps. 66:7).

Let the power of Your anger be released against the powers of darkness (Ps. 90:11).

I release the power and authority of the Lord against all demons I encounter in the name of Jesus (Matt. 10:1).

I am delivered from the power of Satan unto God (Acts 26:18).

Divide the sea, and destroy marine spirits through Your power (Job 26:12).

I am strong in the Lord and in the power of His might (Eph. 6:10).

Cause the powers of darkness to submit to Your power.

Display Your awesome power that men will believe.

Release Your power in healing and deliverance (Luke 5:17).

Release Your powerful voice (Ps. 29:4).

Let me be amazed at Your power (Luke 9:43).

Let great power be released through Your apostles (Acts 4:33).

Let signs, wonders, and miracles be released through
the power of the Holy Spirit (Rom. 15:19).

Let me preach and teach with demonstration
of the Spirit and power (1 Cor. 2:4).

Let Your power work in me (Eph. 3:20).

Release Your powerful angels on my behalf to fight
my battles in the heavens (2 Pet. 2:11; Rev. 18:1).

Release the power of Elijah through Your prophets (Luke 1:17).

Let me be willing in the day of Your power (Ps. 110:3).

RELEASING THE POWER OF THE BLOOD

I cover my mind and thoughts with the blood of Jesus.

I cover my doorpost and possessions with
the blood of Jesus (Exod. 12:13).

I overcome the devil through the blood of Jesus (Rev. 12:11).

I sprinkle the blood of Jesus and receive
multiplied grace and peace (1 Pet. 1:2).

I am made perfect through the blood of the
everlasting covenant (Heb. 13:20–21).

I have boldness to enter into the presence of
God through the blood (Heb. 10:19).

My conscience is purged from dead works to serve the
living God through the blood of Jesus (Heb. 9:14).

I eat the body of Jesus and drink His blood (John 6:54).

I have redemption through the blood of Jesus, and I am redeemed from the power of evil (Eph. 1:7).

I rebuke all spirits of torment and fear because I have peace through the blood of Jesus (Col. 1:20).

I receive the benefits of the new covenant through the blood of Jesus (Matt. 26:28).

I receive healing and health through the blood of Jesus.

I receive abundance and prosperity through the blood of Jesus.

I receive deliverance through the blood of Jesus.

I receive the fullness of the Holy Spirit and the anointing through the blood of Jesus.

The blood of Jesus bears witness to my deliverance and salvation (1 John 5:8).

The blood of Jesus cleanses me from all sin (1 John 1:7).

Jesus resisted unto blood, and His blood gives me victory (Heb. 12:4).

I rebuke and cast out all spirits of guilt, shame, and condemnation through the blood of Jesus.

I break the power of sin and iniquity in my life through the blood of Jesus (Heb. 10:17).

My heart is sprinkled and purified by the blood of Jesus from an evil conscience (Heb. 10:22).

I rebuke Satan, the accuser of the brethren, through the blood of Jesus (Rev. 12:10).

I command all my accusers to depart through the blood of Jesus (John 8:10).

I rebuke and cast out all spirits of slander and accusation through the blood of Jesus (Matt. 12:10).

I release the voice of the blood against demons and evil spirits that would accuse and condemn me (Heb. 12:24).

Warfare Prayers

Lord, teach my hands to war and my fingers to fight (Ps. 144:1).

Lord, I am Your End-Times warrior. Use me as Your weapon against the enemy (2 Chron. 11:1).

The weapons of my warfare are not carnal but mighty through You to the pulling down of strongholds (2 Cor. 10:4).

Satan, you have lost the war in heaven (Rev. 12:7).

Let all the enemies that make war with the Lamb be destroyed (Rev. 17:14).

I do not war after the flesh but after the spirit (2 Cor. 10:3).

Lord, thunder upon the enemy; release Your voice; hail stones and coals of fire (Ps. 18:13).

Send out Your arrows, and scatter them. Shoot out Your light and discomfit them (Ps. 18:14).

Deliver me from my strong enemy, from them that are too strong for me (Ps. 18:17).

Deliver me, and bring me into a large place (Ps. 18:19).

I am your battle-ax and weapon of war (Jer. 51:20).

You have given me the necks of my enemies, and I will destroy them in the name of Jesus (Ps. 18:40).

I am Your anointed, and You give me great deliverance (Ps. 18:50).

I will beat them small as the dust and cast them out as mire in the streets (Ps. 18:42).

I have pursued my enemies and overtaken them. I did not turn until they were consumed (Ps. 18:37).

I have wounded them, and they are not able to rise.
They have fallen under my feet (Ps. 18:38).

I tread upon the lion and adder. The young lion
and dragon I trample underfoot (Ps. 91:13).

I tread upon serpents and scorpions and over all the power of the
enemy, and nothing shall by any means hurt me (Luke 10:19).

I tread down the wicked; they are ashes under my feet (Mal. 4:3).

I will arise and thresh and beat the enemy into pieces (Mic. 4:13).

I rebuke every wild boar of the field in the name of Jesus (Ps. 80:13).

I rebuke every spirit that creeps forth from the forest (Ps. 104:20).

I rebuke every beast of the forest that comes to devour (Isa. 56:9).

I rebuke every lion of the forest that comes to slay (Jer. 5:6).

I close the door to every demonic rat that would attempt
to come into my life in the name of Jesus (Isa. 66:17).

I bind and cast out every thief that would try to steal
my finances in the name of Jesus (John 10:10).

I bind and cast out any spirit that would try
to steal my joy in the name of Jesus.

I bind, expose, and cast out any demon that would try by
stealth (undetected) to come into my life (2 Sam. 19:3).

Lord, cleanse my temple and drive out any
thief from my life (John 2:14–15).

Lord, lift up a standard against any flood the enemy
would try to bring into my life (Isa. 59:19).

I bind and cast out all familiar spirits that would try to
operate in my life in the name of Jesus (Isa. 8:19).

I bind and rebuke any demon that would try to block
my way in the name of Jesus (Matt. 8:28).

I remove all leaven of malice and wickedness
from my life (1 Cor. 5:8).

I rebuke and cast out any froglike spirit from
my life in the name of Jesus (Rev. 16:13).

I bind and rebuke devils in high places in
the name of Jesus (2 Chron. 11:15).

I break off any fellowship with devils through sin, the
flesh, or sacrifice in the name of Jesus (1 Cor. 10:20).

I command all devils to leave my children
in the name of Jesus (Mark 7:29).

Lord, expose any human devils in my life
in the name of Jesus (John 6:70).

Lord, expose any children of the devil that would
try to come into the church (Acts 13:10).

Let every spirit hiding from me be exposed
in the name of Jesus (Josh. 10:16).

Let every hidden snare for my feet be exposed (Jer. 18:22).

I stand against and rebuke every wile of the devil (Eph. 6:11).

I release myself from any snare of the devil
in the name of Jesus (2 Tim. 2:26).

I will not come into the condemnation of the devil (1 Tim. 3:6).

Lord, let no doctrine of the devil be
established in my life (1 Tim. 4:1).

I nullify the power of any sacrifice made to devils in my
city, region, or nation in the name of Jesus (Lev. 17:7).

I bind and rebuke Molech and any spirit that has
been assigned to abort my destiny (Lev. 18:21).

Give me strength to bring forth my destiny (Isa. 66:9).

I overcome every antichrist spirit because greater is He that is in me than he that is in the world (1 John 4:4–5).

I loose myself from every spirit of error in the name of Jesus (1 John 4:6).

Lord, let me not operate in the wrong spirit (Luke 9:55).

I loose myself from every spirit of whoredom in the name of Jesus (Hos. 4:12).

Let me have and walk in an excellent spirit (Dan. 6:3).

I will take heed to my spirit at all times (Mal. 2:15).

I bind and cast out any spirit that would try to tear apart my life in any manner in the name of Jesus (Mark 9:20).

Lord, stir up my spirit to do Your will (Hag. 1:14).

I bind and cast out any demon of slumber from my life in the name of Jesus (Rom. 11:8).

I bind and cast out all demons of fear and timidity in the name of Jesus (2 Tim. 1:7).

I bind and cast out all seducing spirits that would come my way in the name of Jesus (1 Tim. 4:1).

I bind and rebuke the angel of light in the name of Jesus (2 Cor. 11:14).

I reject all false apostolic ministries in the name of Jesus (2 Cor. 11:13).

I reject all false prophetic ministries in the name of Jesus (Matt. 7:15).

I reject all false teaching ministries in the name of Jesus (2 Pet. 2:1).

Expose all false brethren to me (2 Cor. 11:26).

I reject the mouth of vanity and the right hand of falsehood (Ps. 144:8).

I reject every false vision and every false prophetic word released into my life (Jer. 14:14).

I bind Satan, the deceiver, from releasing any deception into my life (Rev. 12:9).

I bind and cast out all spirits of self-deception in the name of Jesus (1 Cor. 3:18).

I bind and cast out any spirit of sorcery that would deceive me in the name of Jesus (Rev. 18:23).

Lord, let no man deceive me (Matt. 24:4).

I bind and rebuke any bewitchment that would keep me from obeying the truth (Gal. 3:1).

I pray for utterance and boldness to make known the mystery of the gospel (Eph. 6:19).

Deliver me out of the hand of wicked and unreasonable men (2 Thess. 3:2).

Evil spirits leave my life as I hear and speak the Word (Matt. 8:16).

I rebuke, still, and cast out the avenger (Ps. 8:2).

I bind and cast out any creeping spirit that would attempt to creep into my life (Ezek. 8:10).

Let the hammer of the wicked be broken (Jer. 50:23).

I renounce all earthly, sensual, and demonic wisdom (James 3:15).

I cast out devils, and I will be perfected (Luke 13:32).

Let every Pharaoh that would pursue my life be drowned in the sea (Exod. 15:4).

I rebuke every demonic bee that would surround me in the name of Jesus (Ps. 118:12).

I bind and cast out any spirit of Absalom that would try to steal my heart from God's ordained leadership (2 Sam. 15:6).

I will sleep well. I will not be kept awake by any spirit of restlessness or insomnia (Ps. 3:5).

I laugh at the enemy through the Holy Spirit (Ps. 2:4).

I cut the cords of the wicked from my life (Ps. 129:4).

Let every cord the enemy tries to put around my life be like burning flax (Judg. 15:14).

I break down every wall of Jericho (Josh. 6:5).

Lord, cleanse my life from secret faults (Ps. 19:12).

Lord, let Your secret be upon my tabernacle (Job 29:4).

Lead me and guide me for Your name's sake (Ps. 31:3).

Guide me continually (Isa. 58:11).

Guide me into all truth (John 16:13).

Guide me with Your eye (Ps. 32:8).

Let me guide my affairs with discretion (Ps. 112:5).

Guide me by the skillfulness of Your hands (Ps. 78:72).

Lead me in a plain path because of my enemies (Ps. 27:11).

Lead me not into temptation, but deliver me from evil (Matt. 6:13).

Lead me, and make Your way straight before my eyes (Ps. 5:8).

Make the crooked places straight and the rough places smooth before me (Isa. 40:4).

Send out Your light and truth, and let them lead me (Ps. 43:3).

Make darkness light before me and crooked things straight (Isa. 42:16).

Teach me to do your will, and lead me into the land of uprightness (Ps. 143:10).

I put on the garment of praise for the spirit of heaviness (Isa. 61:3).

Clothe me with the garment of salvation (Isa. 61:10).

I put on my beautiful garments (Isa. 52:1).

Let my garments always be white (Eccles. 9:8).

Let me be clothed with humility (1 Pet. 5:5).

Cover me with the robe of righteousness (Isa. 61:10).

Let my clothes be full of Your virtue (Mark 5:30).

Let a mantle of power rest upon my life (2 Kings 2:8).

Lord, give me wisdom in every area where I lack (James 1:5).

PRAYERS TO ROOT OUT

Let every plant that my Father has not planted
be rooted out in the name of Jesus.

I lay the ax to the root of every evil tree in my life.

Let every ungodly generational taproot be cut and
pulled out of my bloodline in the name of Jesus.

Let the roots of wickedness be as rottenness.

I speak to every evil tree to be uprooted
and cast into the sea (Luke 17:6).

Let Your holy fire burn up every ungodly
root in the name of Jesus (Mal. 4:1).

Let the confidence of the enemy be rooted out (Job 18:14).

Let every root of bitterness be cut from my life (Heb. 12:15).

Let the prophetic word be released to root
out evil kingdoms (Jer. 1:10).

Let any evil person planted in my church be
rooted out in the name of Jesus.

Let any sickness rooted in my body be
plucked up in the name of Jesus.

Let all false ministries that have rooted
themselves in my city be plucked up.

Let every bramble and nettle be plucked up
from my life in the name of Jesus.

Let all thorns be burned out of my life in
the name of Jesus (Isa. 10:17).

Let all spirits rooted in rejection come out in the name of Jesus.

Let all spirits rooted in pride come out in the name of Jesus.

Let all spirits rooted in rebellion come out in the name of Jesus.

Let all spirits rooted in fear come out in the name of Jesus.

Let all spirits rooted in lust and sexual sin
come out in the name of Jesus.

Let all spirits rooted in curses come out in the name of Jesus.

Let all spirits rooted in witchcraft come out in the name of Jesus.

Let all spirits rooted in any part of my body and
organs come out in the name of Jesus.

PRAYERS AGAINST SATAN (THE DEVIL)

Satan, the Lord rebuke thee (Zech. 3:2).

Get thee hence, Satan, for it is written (Matt. 4:10).

Get behind me, Satan, for it is written (Luke 4:8).

I beheld Satan as lightning fall from heaven (Luke 10:18).

I loose myself from every bond of Satan in
the name of Jesus (Luke 13:16).

Lord, bruise Satan under my feet (Rom. 16:20).

I bind and rebuke all hindering spirits of Satan
in the name of Jesus (1 Thess. 2:18).

I renounce all ungodly anger, and I give
no place to the devil (Eph. 4:27).

I pray to overcome any sifting that Satan would
try to bring into my life (Luke 22:31).

I am delivered from the power of Satan unto God (Acts 26:18).

I bind the thief from stealing, killing, or
destroying in my life (John 10:10).

Lord, remove Satan's seat from my region,
city, and nation (Rev. 2:13).

Lord, remove every synagogue of Satan from
my city, region, and nation (Rev. 3:9).

I bind and rebuke all wrath of the devil
directed against my life (Rev. 12:12).

Devil, I resist you. Flee (James 4:7).

I am sober and vigilant against my
adversary, the devil (1 Pet. 5:8).

Rebuking the Enemy

Satan, the Lord rebukes thee (Zech. 3:2).

Let the enemy perish at Your rebuke, O Lord (Ps. 80:16).

Let the enemy flee at Your rebuke, O Lord (Ps. 104:7).

I rebuke all the winds and storms of the enemy
sent against my life (Mark 4:39).

Rebuke the company of the spearmen and the multitude
of the bulls until they submit (Ps. 68:30).

Rebuke those that rush at me, and let them flee away (Isa. 17:13).

Rebuke the devourer for my sake (Mal. 3:11).

Rebuke the horse and chariot, and let them
fall into a deep sleep (Ps. 76:6).

I rebuke every unclean spirit that would attempt
to operate in my life (Luke 9:42).

I rebuke the proud spirits that are cursed (Ps. 119:21).

I release furious rebukes upon the enemy (Ezek. 25:17).

Let the blast of your nostrils rebuke the enemy (2 Sam. 22:16).

Rebuke the enemy with flames of fire (Isa. 66:15).

Let a thousand flee at my rebuke, O Lord (Isa. 30:17).

Rebuke every sea that would try to close upon my life (Ps. 106:9).

Devil, I rebuke you. Hold your peace, and come out (Mark 1:25).

SPEAKING TO MOUNTAINS

I speak to every mountain in my life and command it
to be removed and cast into the sea (Mark 11:23).

I speak to every financial mountain to be removed
from my life in the name of Jesus.

Let every evil mountain hear the voice of the
Lord and be removed (Mic. 6:2).

I prophesy to the mountains and command them to hear
the Word of the Lord and be removed (Ezek. 36:4).

Let the mountains tremble at the presence of God (Hab. 3:10).

I contend with every mountain and command
them to hear my voice (Mic. 6:1).

Lay the mountain of Esau (the flesh) to waste (Mal. 1:3).

Put forth Your hand, O Lord, and overturn
the mountains by the roots (Job 28:9).

I speak to every mountain of debt to be
removed and cast into the sea.

Lord, You are against every destroying mountain (Jer. 51:25).

Let the mountains melt at Your presence, O God (Judg. 5:5).

Make waste the evil mountains in my life, O Lord (Isa. 42:15).

I thresh every mountain, I beat them small, and
I make the hills as chaff (Isa. 41:15).

Every mountain in my way will become a plain (Zech. 4:7).

RELEASING THE SPOILERS

Let the counsel of the wicked be spoiled (Job 12:17).

Lead the princes of darkness away spoiled (Job 12:19).

Let the stouthearted be spoiled (Ps. 76:5).

I bind the enemy, strip him of his armor,
and divide his spoils (Luke 11:22).

I release the spoilers to come upon Babylon
and destroy her (Jer. 51:53).

I release the spoilers to come upon the high
places in the name of Jesus (Jer. 12:12).

Lord, You have spoiled principalities and powers (Col. 2:15).

I spoil the enemy and take back his goods
in the name of Jesus (Exod. 12:36).

I spoil the tents of the enemy in the name of Jesus (1 Sam. 17:53).

I spoil those that have attempted to spoil me (Ezek. 39:10).

The enemy will not spoil me, but he will be spoiled (Isa. 33:1).

Let the palaces and headquarters of darkness be
spoiled in the name of Jesus (Amos 3:11).

Let the proud spirits be spoiled in the name of Jesus (Zech. 11:3).

I release the cankerworm to spoil the works of
darkness in the name of Jesus (Nah. 3:16).

Let the fortresses of darkness be spoiled in
the name of Jesus (Hos. 10:14).

SECTION 3

CONFRONTING the ENEMY'S TACTICS

WE ARE NOT TO BE IGNORANT OF THE DEVIL'S TACTICS. We can overcome all the schemes of the devil. The devil is a schemer. A *scheme* is a plan, design, or program of action. The Bible talks about the wiles of the devil (Eph. 6:11). A *wile* is a trick or a trap. A *trap* is a snare.

Warfare involves tactics and strategies. The greatest generals are great tacticians and strategists. You cannot win without a strategy. Don't allow the enemy to strategize against you. Overcome and destroy his strategies through prayer.

Traps and snares are hidden. People fall into traps unknowingly. We are delivered from the snare of the fowler. A *fowler* is a hunter. Satan is the hunter of souls. We can release ourselves and others through prayer.

The main tactic of the enemy is deception. He is a liar and the father of lies. The Word of God exposes the tactics of the enemy. God is light, and His Word is light. The light exposes the enemy and tears away the darkness.

Multitudes of people are deceived by the enemy. There are hosts of lying and deceiving spirits that work under the authority of Satan. These spirits include delusion, deception, lying, seducing, blinding, error, and guile. Our praying can strip the power of these deceiving spirits and cause the eyes of people to be opened.

45

David prayed against the enemy conspiracies of the wicked. The Psalms are filled with references to the plans of his enemies to overthrow him. His prayers were the key in destroying these plans and bringing him deliverance. David prayed for his enemies to be scattered, confused, exposed, and destroyed.

David's struggles were with natural enemies. Behind these natural enemies were spiritual ones that were opposed to the Davidic kingdom. Jesus was to come from this line and sit upon this throne. David was fighting something beyond the natural. Through the Holy Spirit he was contending with the powers of darkness that were set against the arrival of the kingdom of God.

These powers were also manifested through Herod, who attempted to kill the coming Messiah. Herod was driven by spirits of fear and murder. He was used by Satan to attempt to abort the coming kingdom. However, the Holy Spirit had already been loosed through the prayers of David, and David's throne was secure.

Many of these warfare prayers are taken from the psalms of David. Jesus is the Son of David. He sits on the throne of David. David's prophetic prayers were weapons against the enemy's attempt to stop the promised seed. David's victories in prayer opened the way for his throne to continue. The throne of wickedness was unable to overcome the throne of righteousness.

God taught David. He became the warrior king. His victories caused his kingdom to be established. His victory over the house of Saul came after a long war (2 Sam. 3:1). Don't become discouraged in prayer. Continue to pray. You will become stronger, and the enemy will become weaker.

David consumed his enemies (Ps. 18:37–40). He did not turn until they were destroyed. We must see our spiritual enemies completely destroyed. We must pursue the enemy. To *pursue* means to follow in order to overtake or capture. It means to chase with hostile intent. We cannot be passive when it comes to warfare.

David's victories prepared the way for Solomon. Solomon enjoyed peace and prosperity. Solomon's name means "peace." *Peace* is the Hebrew word *shalom*. *Shalom* means "peace, prosperity, favor, health, and well-being." Your victories over the enemy will release *shalom*. You will experience greater levels of peace and prosperity.

QUENCHING THE FIRE OF THE ENEMY

I quench with the shield of faith every fiery dart
the enemy sends my way (Eph. 6:16).

I quench every fiery dart of jealousy, envy, anger, bitterness,
and rage sent against my life in the name of Jesus.

I quench every firebrand sent against my life by
the enemy in the name of Jesus (Isa. 7:4).

I bind and rebuke all spirits of jealousy directed
against my life in the name of Jesus.

I quench every fire the enemy would throw into my
sanctuary in the name of Jesus (Ps. 74:7).

I bind and cast out every fiery serpent sent against
my life in the name of Jesus (Isa. 30:6).

I quench every burning lamp that comes from
the leviathan's mouth (Job 41:19).

I will not be burned by the fire of the enemy (Isa. 43:2).

I overcome every fiery trial sent against
my life by the enemy (1 Pet. 1:7).

The enemy will not be able to burn up my harvest (2 Sam. 14:30).

I quench every fire of wickedness sent against
my life in the name of Jesus (Isa. 9:18).

I quench all ungodly words spoken against my
life in the name of Jesus (Prov. 16:27).

I quench every torch the enemy would use against
my life in the name of Jesus (Zech. 12:6).

I quench all gossip directed against my life
in the name of Jesus (Prov. 26:20).

The enemy's flame will not kindle upon me (Isa. 43:2).

BREAKING CURSES AND RELEASING THE BLESSINGS OF GOD

I am redeemed from the curse through the blood of Jesus (Gal. 3:13).

I am the seed of Abraham, and his blessing is mine (Gal. 3:14).

I choose blessing instead of cursing and life instead of death (Deut. 11:26).

I break and release myself from all generational curses and iniquities as a result of the sins of my ancestors in the name of Jesus.

I break and release myself from all curses on both sides of my family back sixty generations.

I break all curses of witchcraft, sorcery, and divination in the name of Jesus.

I break and release myself from all curses of pride and rebellion in the name of Jesus.

I break and release myself from all curses of death and destruction in the name of Jesus.

I break and rebuke all curses of sickness and infirmity in the name of Jesus.

I break and release myself from all curses of poverty, lack, and debt in the name of Jesus.

I break and release myself from all curses of rejection in the name of Jesus.

I break and release myself from all curses of doublemindedness and schizophrenia in the name of Jesus.

I break and release myself from all curses of Jezebel and Ahab in the name of Jesus.

I break and release myself from all curses of divorce and separation in the name of Jesus.

I break and release myself from all curses of lust
and perversion in the name of Jesus.

I break and release myself from all curses of confusion
and mental illness in the name of Jesus.

I break and release myself from all curses
of idolatry in the name of Jesus.

I break and release myself from all curses causing
accidents and premature death in the name of Jesus.

I break and release myself from all curses of
wandering and vagabond in the name of Jesus.

I break and release myself from all spoken curses
and negative words spoken against me by others
and by those in authority, and I bless them.

I break and release myself from all self-inflicted curses by
negative words I have spoken in the name of Jesus.

I command every demon hiding and operating behind
a curse to come out in the name of Jesus.

PRAYERS TO OVERCOME SATANIC AND DEMONIC CONSPIRACIES

I loose confusion against every satanic and
demonic conspiracy against my life.

Let the secret counsel of the wicked be turned into foolishness.

Let those gathered against me be scattered.

Send out Your lightning, O Lord, and scatter the enemy.

Destroy, O Lord, and divide their tongues (Ps. 55:9).

No weapon formed against me shall prosper. The gates
and plans of hell shall not prevail against me.

I overcome every strategy of hell against my life.

Every strategy of hell is exposed and brought to light.

I receive the plans of God for my life, thoughts of peace and not evil to bring me to an expected end.

I am delivered from every satanic trap and plot against my life.

I release the whirlwind to scatter those who would conspire against me.

Let those who devise my hurt be turned back and brought to confusion.

Let the nets they have hid catch themselves, and into that very destruction let them fall.

I bind and rebuke every spirit of Sanballat and Tobiah in the name of Jesus (Neh. 6:1–6).

Hide me from the secret counsel of the wicked (Ps. 64:2).

OVERCOMING AND DIVIDING DEMONIC CONFEDERACIES

I break and divide every demonic confederacy against my life in the name of Jesus.

I loose confusion into every demonic confederacy directed against my life, family, and church in the name of Jesus.

Divide and scatter them that are joined together against me.

I bind and rebuke all demonic reinforcements sent by Satan to attack my life.

Make the ruling spirits of these confederacies be like Oreb, Zeeb, Zebah, and Zalmunna (Ps. 83:5–11).

O my God, make them like the wheel, as the stubble before the wind (Ps. 83:13).

Persecute them with Thy tempest, and make them afraid with Thy storm (Ps. 83:15).

Let them be confounded and troubled forever. Let them be put to shame and perish (Ps. 83:17).

Loose confusion, and let them attack each other in the name of Jesus (2 Chron. 20:23).

PRAYERS OVER HIGH PLACES

Lord, You created the high places for Your glory. Let not the enemy control the high places.

I bind the prince of the power of the air (Eph. 2:2).

I bind the powers of darkness that would control the airwaves and release filth, violence, and witchcraft through the media in the name of Jesus.

I take authority over the princes of media in the name of Jesus (Dan. 8:20).

I bind spiritual wickedness in high places (Eph. 6:12).

Lord, destroy the idols in high places (Lev. 26:30).

I pluck down the high places of the enemy (Num. 33:52).

I am a king, and I break down the high places in the name of Jesus (2 Kings 18:4).

I remove Nehushtan (previous moves of God that have become idols) from the high places (2 Kings 18:4).

I remove the religious spirits from the high places (2 Kings 23:8).

Let the high place of Tophet be removed (Jer. 7:31).

Let Your holy fire burn up the high places.

Let the high places of witchcraft be destroyed in the name of Jesus (2 Chron. 28:4).

Destroy all false worship in the high places (2 Chron. 28:25).

Let the high places be purged through Your anointing (2 Chron. 34:3).

Remove every false ministry in high places (1 Kings 12:31).

Remove all strange gods from the high places (2 Chron. 14:3).

Remove every satanic altar erected in the high places (2 Chron. 14:3).

Let all high places established by any ungodly ruler be removed in the name of Jesus (2 Kings 23:19).

Let all the high places of Baal be broken down (Jer. 19:5).

I prophesy to the ancient high places and dispossess the enemy (Ezek. 36:1–3).

Let righteous men with Your wisdom sit in the high governmental places of my city and nation (Prov. 9:3).

I will walk upon the high places (Hab. 3:19).

Let every high place of wickedness that has not been removed be removed (1 Kings 15:14).

Let me ride upon the high places of the earth, and let me eat the increase of the fields, and let me suck honey out of the rock and oil out of the flinty rock (Deut. 32:13).

Let all high places built by my ancestors be removed (2 Kings 18:4).

Let not the high places our spiritual fathers destroyed be rebuilt (2 Chron. 33:3).

Let the high places be desolate (Ezek. 6:6).

I tread upon the high places of the wicked (Deut. 33:29).

I break the power of any sacrifice done in the high places (1 Kings 3:2).

I walk in the spirit of Josiah to deal with the high places (2 Chron. 34:3).

Lord, open rivers in high places (Isa. 41:18).

PRAYERS OVER GATES

Through Jesus let me possess the gate of the enemy (Gen. 22:17).

Establish the gates of praise in my life (Isa. 60:18).

I release battering rams against the gates of hell (Ezek. 21:22).

The gates of hell cannot prevail against me (Matt. 16:18).

Let the gates of my life and city be open
to the King of glory (Ps. 24:7).

Open to me the gates of righteousness
that I may enter in (Ps. 118:19).

Strengthen the bars of my gates (Ps. 147:13).

Break the gates of brass, and cut in sunder
the bars of iron (Isa. 45:2).

Open before me the gates, that I may go in and receive the treasure
of darkness and hidden riches of secret places (Isa. 45:1–3).

I rebuke every enemy in the gates (Ps. 127:5).

Let all the gates of my life and city be
repaired through the Holy Spirit.

Let the valley gate be repaired (Neh. 2:13).

Let the gate of the fountain (represents the flow
of the Holy Spirit) be repaired (Neh. 2:14).

Let the sheep gate (represents the apostolic) be repaired (Neh. 3:1).

Let the fish gate (represents evangelism) be repaired (Neh. 3:3).

Let the old gate (represents moves of the
past) be repaired (Neh. 3:6).

Let the dung gate (represents deliverance) be repaired (Neh. 3:14).

Let the water gate (represents preaching and
teaching) be repaired (Neh. 3:26).

Let the east gate (represents the glory) be
repaired (Neh. 3:29; Ezek. 43:1–2).

Let the waters flow through the utter gate into my life, past
my ankles, past my loins, and past my neck (Ezek. 47:1–5).

Make my gates of carbuncles (Isa. 54:12).

My gates will be open continually to receive blessings (Isa. 60:11).

I command the north gate, the south gate, the east gate, and
the west gate to open in my city to the King of glory.

I rebuke all enemies that would stand at the gates
and try to stop salvation from entering in.

I pray for the apostolic gatekeepers of my city
to arise and take their place (Lam. 5:14).

Let the gates of my life and city be shut to uncleanness, witchcraft,
drugs, perversion, and wickedness in the name of Jesus.

I pray for the gateway cities in my nation to become
gateways of righteousness and not iniquity.

Lord, raise up bethel churches that will be
the gate of heaven (Gen. 28:17).

Lord, raise up apostolic gate churches that will
usher presence and revelation into my region.

PRAYERS AGAINST IDOLS

Let any idol in my life or nation be destroyed and
burned with Your fire (1 Kings 15:13).

Lord, cut down all the idols in the land (2 Chron. 34:7).

Let the familiar spirits, wizards, and idols be
taken out of the land (2 Kings 23:24).

Let the idols be confounded and the images
be broken in pieces (Jer. 50:2).

Let men throw away their idols and turn to You, O Lord (Isa. 31:7).

I renounce all idolatry in my bloodline and break all curses of idolatry in the name of Jesus (2 Kings 21:21).

Lord, put the names of the idols out of the land (Zech. 13:2).

I will keep myself from idols (1 John 5:21).

Abolish the idols in America and the nations (Isa. 2:18).

Lord, expose all idols as lying vanities (Zech. 10:2).

I renounce all covetousness; I will not serve the god of mammon (Col. 3:5).

Let Babylon, the mother of harlots and abominations of the earth, fall in the name of Jesus (Rev. 17:5).

Lord, cleanse the pollution of idols from the land (Acts 15:20).

Sprinkle clean water upon me, and cleanse me from all filthiness, and cleanse me from all idols (Ezek. 36:25).

Let me not go astray after any idol (Ezek. 44:10).

Let all false gods and idols (including humans) be removed from my life in the name of Jesus.

I will put no other gods before You, Lord (Exod. 20:3).

PRAYERS THAT DESTROY OPPRESSION

I rebuke and cast out any spirit that would attempt to oppress me in the name of Jesus.

Jesus, You went about doing good and healing all those oppressed of the devil (Acts 10:38).

I strip all power from spirits that would oppress me (Eccles. 4:1).

I rebuke and cast out all spirits of poverty that would oppress me (Eccles. 5:8).

I rebuke all spirits of madness and confusion that would attempt to oppress my mind in the name of Jesus (Eccles. 7:7).

O Lord, undertake for me against all my oppressors (Isa. 38:14).

Lord, You are my refuge from the oppressor (Ps. 9:9).

Deliver me from the wicked that would oppress me and from my deadly enemies that would surround me (Ps. 17:9).

Deliver me from oppressors that seek after my soul (Ps. 54:3).

Break in pieces the oppressor (Ps. 72:4).

I rebuke and cast out all spirits of affliction, sorrow, and anything attempting to bring me low in the name of Jesus (Ps. 107:39).

Leave me not to my oppressors (Ps. 119:121).

Let not the proud oppress me (Ps. 119:122).

Deliver me from the oppression of men (Ps. 119:134).

I rule over my oppressors (Ps. 14:2).

Let the oppressors be consumed out of the land (Isa. 16:4).

I rebuke the voice of the oppressor in the name of Jesus (Ps. 55:3).

I am established in righteousness, and I am far from oppression (Isa. 54:14).

Punish those who attempt to oppress me (Jer. 30:20).

The enemy will not take my inheritance through oppression (Ezek. 46:18).

Execute judgment against my oppressors (Ps. 146:7).

BREAKING THE POWER OF SCHIZOPHRENIA AND DOUBLEMINDEDNESS

(Based on the schizophrenia revelation of Ida Mae Hammond.)

I bind and rebuke every spirit that would attempt to distort, disturb, or disintegrate the development of my personality in the name of Jesus.

I break all curses of schizophrenia and doublemindedness on my family in the name of Jesus.

I bind and rebuke the spirit of doublemindedness in the name of Jesus (James 1:8).

I bind and take authority over the strongmen of rejection and rebellion and separate them in the name of Jesus.

I bind and cast out the spirits of rejection, fear of rejection, and self-rejection in the name of Jesus.

I bind and cast out all spirits of lust, fantasy lust, harlotry, and perverseness in the name of Jesus.

I bind and cast out all spirits of insecurity and inferiority in the name of Jesus.

I bind and cast out all spirits of self-accusation and compulsive confession in the name of Jesus.

I bind and cast out all spirits of fear of judgment, self-pity, false compassion, and false responsibility in the name of Jesus.

I bind and cast out all spirits of depression, despondency, despair, discouragement, and hopelessness in the name of Jesus.

I bind and cast out all spirits of guilt, condemnation, unworthiness, and shame in the name of Jesus.

I bind and cast out all spirits of perfection, pride, vanity, ego, intolerance, frustration, and impatience in the name of Jesus.

I bind and cast out all spirits of unfairness, withdrawal, pouting, unreality, fantasy, daydreaming, and vivid imagination in the name of Jesus.

I bind and cast out all spirits of self-awareness, timidity, loneliness, and sensitivity in the name of Jesus.

I bind and cast out all spirits of talkativeness, nervousness, tension, and fear in the name of Jesus.

I bind and cast out all spirits of self-will, selfishness, and stubbornness in the name of Jesus.

I bind and cast out the spirit of accusation in the name of Jesus.

I bind and cast out all spirits of self-delusion, self-deception, and self-seduction in the name of Jesus.

I bind and cast out all spirits of judgment, pride, and unteachableness in the name of Jesus.

I bind and cast out all spirits of control and possessiveness in the name of Jesus.

I bind and cast out the root of bitterness in the name of Jesus.

I bind and cast out all spirits of hatred, resentment, violence, murder, unforgiveness, anger, and retaliation in the name of Jesus.

I bind and cast out spirits of paranoia, suspicion, distrust, persecution, confrontation, and fear in the name of Jesus.

PRAYERS AND DECREES THAT BREAK THE POWERS OF DARKNESS

Let the Assyrian be broken in my land (Isa. 14:25).

Break in pieces the gates of brass, and cut the bars of iron (Isa. 45:2).

I break every yoke from off my neck, and I burst all the bonds in the name of Jesus (Jer. 30:8).

Break them with the rod of iron, and dash them
in pieces like a potter's vessel (Ps. 2:9).

Break the arm of the wicked (Ps. 10:15).

Break their teeth, O God, in their mouths. Break
the teeth of the young lions (Ps. 58:6).

Let the oppressor be broken in pieces (Ps. 72:4).

Let the arms of the wicked be broken (Ps. 37:17).

Let the horns of the wicked be broken (Dan. 8:8).

Let the kingdoms of darkness be broken (Dan. 11:4).

Let the foundations of the wicked be broken (Ezek. 30:4).

Let the kingdoms of Babylon be broken (Jer. 51:58).

Let all the bows of the wicked be broken (Ps. 37:14).

I break in pieces the horse and the rider (Jer. 51:21).

I break in pieces the chariot and the rider (Jer. 51:21).

I break in pieces the captains and the rulers (Jer. 51:23).

Let Your Word out of my mouth be like a hammer
that breaks the rocks in pieces (Jer. 23:29).

Break down every wall erected by the enemy
against my life (Ezek. 13:14).

I break down every altar erected by the enemy against
my life in the name of Jesus (Hos. 10:2).

Let the idols and images of the land be broken
by Your power, O Lord (Deut. 7:5).

I break and disannul every demonic covenant made
by my ancestors in the name of Jesus (Isa. 28:18).

PRAYERS AGAINST THE SPIRIT OF DESTRUCTION

I bind and cast out the spirit of Apollyon
(Abaddon) in the name of Jesus (Rev. 9:11).

I am redeemed from destruction (Ps. 103:4).

I break all curses of destruction in my family
and bloodline in the name of Jesus.

I renounce all pride that would open the
door for destruction (Prov. 16:18).

Rescue my soul from destructions (Ps. 35:17).

Send Your Word, and deliver me from
any destruction (Ps. 107:20).

The destroyer cannot come into my life or family
in the name of Jesus (Exod. 12:23).

The destroyer cannot destroy my prosperity (Job 15:21).

I am delivered from destruction that wastes at noonday (Ps. 91:6).

There is no wasting or destruction within my borders (Isa. 60:18).

I will enter in at the straight gate, and I will not walk
in the path that leads to destruction (Matt. 7:13).

I bind the spirit of mammon that leads
to destruction (1 Tim. 6:9–10).

I will keep my mouth and avoid destruction (Prov. 18:7).

I bind and rebuke the spirit of poverty that
leads to destruction (Prov. 10:15).

I rebuke all destruction from my gates in
the name of Jesus (Isa. 24:12).

CLOSING BREACHES AND HEDGES

I close up any breach in my life that would give Satan and
demons access in the name of Jesus (Eccles. 10:8).

I pray for every broken hedge in my life to be
restored in the name of Jesus (Eccles. 10:8).

I stand in the gap and make up the hedge (Ezek. 22:30).

I repent and receive forgiveness for any sin that has opened the
door for any spirit to enter and operate in my life (Eph. 4:27).

I am a rebuilder of the wall and a repairer of the breach (Isa. 58:12).

I renounce all crooked speech that would cause a
breach in the name of Jesus (Prov. 15:4).

Bind up all my breaches, O Lord (Isa. 30:26).

Let every breach be stopped in the name of Jesus (Neh. 4:7).

Let my walls be salvation and my gates praise (Isa. 60:18).

I pray for a hedge of protection around my mind, body,
finances, possessions, and family in the name of Jesus.

Destroying Evil Cauldrons (Pots)

I rebuke and destroy every wicked cauldron
in the name of Jesus (Ezek. 11:11–12).

I rebuke and destroy every seething pot or cauldron stirred
up by the enemy against my life, city, or nation (Job 41:20).

Let every wicked cauldron in my city be
broken in the name of Jesus.

I break every witchcraft cauldron stirred up by
witches and warlocks in the name of Jesus.

Lord, visit every witch and warlock in my region, and
convict. Let them repent, turn to You, and be saved.

I am delivered from the boiling pot in the
name of Jesus (Ezek. 24:1–5).

Lord, bring me out of the midst of every cauldron (Ezek. 11:7).

The enemy will not eat my flesh, break my bones, and put me in his cauldron (Mic. 3:3).

Lord, deliver and protect me from every pot of evil in the name of Jesus (Jer. 1:13–14).

Lord, deliver me from the boiling pot of pride (Job 41:31).

DESTROYING YOKES AND REMOVING BURDENS

I remove all false burdens placed on me by people, leaders, or churches in the name of Jesus (1 Thess. 2:6).

I remove all heavy burdens placed on my life by the enemy in the name of Jesus.

Let your anointing break the enemy's burden from off my neck, and let every yoke be destroyed (Isa. 10:27).

Remove my shoulder from every burden (Ps. 81:6).

I cast my cares upon the Lord (1 Pet. 5:7).

I cast my burdens upon the Lord, and He sustains me (Ps. 55:22).

Lord, break the yoke of the enemy's burden, and break the staff and the rod of the oppressor as in the day of Midian (Isa. 9:4).

Let every yoke of poverty be destroyed in the name of Jesus.

Let every yoke of sickness be destroyed in the name of Jesus.

Let every yoke of bondage be destroyed in the name of Jesus (Gal. 5:1).

Let every unequal yoke be broken in the name of Jesus (2 Cor. 6:14).

I destroy every yoke and burden of religion and legalism on my life by religious leaders in the name of Jesus (Matt. 23:4).

Let every burdensome stone be released from my life in the name of Jesus (Zech. 12:3).

I take upon my life the yoke and burden of Jesus (Matt. 11:30).

SECTION 4

DESTROYING the ENEMY'S FORCES

JESUS CAME TO DESTROY THE WORKS OF THE DEVIL (1 John 3:8). THE works of the devil are carried out by his forces. Satan's kingdom consists of principalities, powers, rulers of the darkness of this world, and spiritual wickedness in high places. There are different kinds of demons and different levels of wickedness. We can destroy the wicked early (Ps. 101:8). We can destroy them that hate us (Ps. 18:40).

Satan is rendered helpless when his forces are destroyed. We have authority to bind the strongman and strip him of his armor. Israel was sent into Canaan to destroy different nations, which are pictures of kingdoms that possessed the land. Each kingdom represented a different type of stronghold God wanted His people to destroy.

Demons are also represented by different creatures. The diversity in the animal kingdom is a picture of the diversity in the kingdom of darkness. The Bible talks about serpents, scorpions, lions, jackals, bulls, foxes, owls, sea serpents, flies, and dogs. These represent different kinds of evil spirits that operate to destroy mankind. They are invisible to the natural eye. They are just as real, however, as natural creatures.

We must always remember that there are more with us than against us. The forces of light are far superior to the forces of darkness. Jesus is the Lord of the armies. The armies of heaven are fighting with the armies of earth. Releasing the angelic armies of heaven is an important strategy in warfare.

We can destroy and rout the forces of darkness in the heavens, the earth, the sea, and under the earth. These forces can operate through people, governments, economic systems, educational systems, and different structures set up by men. These forces can operate from different locations and in different territories.

The idols that men worship are made in the image of men, four-footed beasts, birds, and creeping things. Behind these idols are demons. These are evil spirits that manifest in the natural through idols. These gods (idols) were also male and female. The nations worshiped gods and goddesses. Jezebel is an example of a female principality.

The Bible uses strong words that pertain to warfare including:

- *Abolish*—to end, cut, strike through (Isa. 2:18; 2 Tim. 1:10)

- *Beat down*—beat, bruise, violently strike, crush, destroy, discomfort, break down by violence, dismay, terrify (Judg. 9:45; 2 Kings 13:25; Ps. 18:42; Isa. 27:12; Jer. 46:5)

- *Break down*—deliver, break, rend in pieces, crush, destroy, to spoil (by breaking in pieces), pluck down, pull down, ruin, beat down, cast down, dash in pieces, disperse (Exod. 34:13; Lev. 26:19; Ps. 2:9; 10:15; 58:6; 72:4; Eccles. 3:3; Isa. 45:2; Jer. 28:4; Dan. 2:40)

- *Cast down*—to tear down, break down, destroy, overthrow, pull down, throw down, cast down to hell (Judg. 6:28, 30; Ps. 17:13; 89:44; 102:10; 147:6; Isa. 28:2; Jer. 8:12; Dan. 7:9; 8:10; 2 Cor. 4:9; 10:5; 2 Pet. 2:4)

- *Cast out*—to occupy by driving out the previous tenants and possessing their place, to seize, to rob, to inherit, to expel, to impoverish, to send away, to push away or down, cast away, to banish, to eject, send out, throw out (Exod. 34:24; Lev. 18:24; Deut. 6:19; 1 Kings 14:24; 2 Kings 16:3; Job 20:15; Ps. 5:10; Matt. 12:28; Mark 6:13; Luke 9:40; John 12:31; Rev. 12:9)

- *Chase (pursue)*—run after with hostile intent, put to flight, persecute (Lev. 26:7–8; Deut. 32:30; Ps. 18:37; 35:3; Isa. 17:13)

- *Confound (confuse)*—to be ashamed, disappointed, brought to confusion, put to shame (Ps. 35:4, 26; 40:14; 70:2, 13, 24; 83:17; 97:7; 109:29; 129:5; Jer. 17:18; 50:2)

- *Consume*—to end, consume away, destroy, make clean riddance, to eat up, devour, burn up (Deut. 7:16, 22; Ps. 37:20; 71:13; 104:35; 2 Thess. 2:8; Heb. 12:29)

- *Contend*—to grate, to anger, meddle, strive, stir up, grapple with, to defend, chide, rebuke, initiate a controversy (Deut. 2:24; Isa. 41:12; 49:25; Jer. 12:5; Jude 9)

- *Destroy*—to end, to cease, destroy utterly, make clean, waste, make accursed, tear down, beat down, break down, to devour, eat up (Lev. 26:30, 44; 20:17; 31:3; Ps. 5:6, 10; 18:40; 21:10; 28:5; 52:5; 55:9; 74:8; 101:8; 144:6; Prov. 15:25; Isa. 23:11; Jer. 1:10; Matt. 21:41; Mark 1:24; 9:22; John 10:10; 1 John 3:8)

- *Fight*—to consume, to battle, make war, overcome, prevail, struggle, contend with the adversary (Exod. 14:14; 17:9; Deut. 1:30; Josh. 10:25; Judg. 1:1, 3, 9;

Ps. 35:1; 144:1; Dan. 10:20; 1 Tim. 6:12; 2 Tim. 4:7; Heb. 10:32)

- *Prevail*—to enclose, to hold back, shut up, stop, be strong, put on strength, to overpower, restrain, bind, conquer (2 Chron. 14:11; Ps. 9:19; Isa. 42:13; Matt. 16:18)

- *Smite*—strike, beat, cast forth, slaughter, give stripes, wound, slay, push, defeat, inflict, dash, gore, hurt, put to the worse (Num. 25:17; Deut. 13:15; Josh. 7:3; Judg. 20:31; 1 Sam. 15:3; Isa. 19:22; Jer. 43:11; Acts 7:24; Rev. 11:6)

- *Wrestle*—to struggle, grapple (Gen. 30:8; 32:24; Eph. 6:12)

The Bible contains many words that speak of warfare. The Bible is filled with warfare. The history of man has been determined by wars. John saw war in heaven between Michael and his angels and Satan and his angels (Rev. 12:7). War requires warriors. Warriors must have the tenacity to overcome their enemies. Remember, God trains our hands to war and our fingers to fight (Ps. 144:1).

PRAYERS AGAINST DEMONIC PRINCES

Jesus, You have cast out the prince of this world and defeated him (John 12:31).

Jesus, You spoiled principalities and made an open show of them (Col. 2:15).

I bind the prince of the power of the air in the name of Jesus (Eph. 2:2).

I bind and rebuke Beelzebub, the prince of demons (Matt. 12:24).

I bind the principalities and powers in my region in the name of Jesus (Eph. 6:12).

I command the principalities to come down in the name of Jesus (Jer. 13:18).

Lord, release Your warrior angels against the demonic princes (Dan. 10:20).

Smite the princes as the days of old (Josh. 13:21).

Bring the iniquity of every profane prince to an end, and remove the diadem from his head (Ezek. 21:25–26).

Lead the princes away spoiled, and overthrow the mighty (Job 12:19).

Make the nobles like Oreb and like Zeeb, and all their princes like Zebah and Zalmunna (Ps. 83:11).

Pour contempt upon the demon princes (Ps. 107:40).

Cut off the spirits of princes (Ps. 76:12).

I rebuke and bind all princes that would speak against me (Ps. 119:23).

I rebuke and bind all princes that would persecute me (Ps. 119:161).

Bring the princes to nothing (Isa. 34:12).

Punish the princes with Your power (Zeph. 1:8).

PRAYERS AGAINST LEVIATHAN AND MARINE SPIRITS

O Lord, break the heads of the dragons in the waters (Ps. 74:13).

Cut off the head of every hydra in the name of Jesus.

Break the heads of leviathan in pieces (Ps. 74:14).

Punish leviathan, the piercing serpent, even leviathan the crooked serpent, with Your sore, great, and strong sword (Isa. 27:1).

Slay the dragon that is in the sea (Ps. 27:1).

I break all curses of pride and leviathan from my life in the name of Jesus.

Rip the scales of leviathan (Job 41:15).

Break the strength of leviathan's neck (Ps. 18:40).

Break the stony heart of leviathan and crush it to pieces (Job 41:24).

Break the teeth of leviathan and pluck the spoil out of his mouth (Job 41:15).

I put a hook in leviathan's nose, a cord around his tongue, and I bore a thorn in his jaw (Job 41:1–2).

Lord, You rule the sea and the waters by Your strength.

Do not let any evil waters overflow my life.

The channels of waters are seen at Your rebuke (Ps. 18:15).

Rebuke all proud and arrogant demons that are cursed (Ps. 119:21).

I bind every sea monster that would attack my life or region in the name of Jesus (Lam. 4:3).

Bring down the haughty demons by Your power.

Bring down the proud demons that have exalted themselves against Your people.

Scatter the proud in the imagination of their hearts.

God, You resist the proud. Your power is against the high ones who have rebelled against You.

Let not the foot of pride come against me (Ps. 36:11).

Break the crown of pride (Isa. 28:1).

Break Rahab in pieces, as one that is slain. Scatter Your enemies with Your strong arm (Ps. 89:10).

Let not leviathan oppress me (Ps. 119:122).

O Lord, render a reward to leviathan (Ps. 94:2).

Raise up a watch over leviathan (Job 7:12).

Let not the proud waters go over my soul (Ps. 124:5).

I rebuke and destroy every trap the devil has set for me (Ps. 140:5).

Let the proud spirits stumble and fall (Jer. 50:32).

Break the pride of leviathan's power (Lev. 26:19).

Awake, awake. Put on strength, O arm of the Lord. I command the helpers of Rahab to bow before the Lord (Isa. 51:9).

Let not the foot of pride come against me (Ps. 36:11).

I strip the scales of leviathan and take away his armor (Job 41:15; Luke 11:22).

Cast abroad the rage of thy wrath and abase leviathan (Job 40:11).

Smite through leviathan with your understanding (Job 26:12).

Look on leviathan, and bring him low. Tread him down in his place (Job 40:12).

Rebuke the bulls of Bashan (Ps. 22:12).

Let the mighty be spoiled; let the oaks of Bashan howl (Zech. 11:2).

Bring Your people from Bashan; bring Your people from the depths of the sea (Ps. 68:22).

Smite Bashan and the kingdom of Og (Ps. 135:10–11).

I bind and cast out all mind-control spirits of the octopus and squid in the name of Jesus.

Let the waters of the deep be dried up, and destroy every spirit of leviathan (Job 41:31; Isa. 44:27).

In the name of Jesus, I dry up your rivers, your seas, and your springs (Isa. 19:5).

I call for a drought upon leviathan's waters (Jer. 50:38; Jer. 51:36).

Prayers Against Jezebel

I loose the hounds of heaven against Jezebel (1 Kings 21:23).

I rebuke and bind the spirits of witchcraft, lust, seduction, intimidation, idolatry, and whoredom connected to Jezebel.

I release the spirit of Jehu against Jezebel and her cohorts (2 Kings 9:30–33).

I command Jezebel to be thrown down and eaten by the hounds of heaven.

I rebuke all spirits of false teaching, false prophecy, idolatry, and perversion connected with Jezebel (Rev. 2:20).

I loose tribulation against the kingdom of Jezebel (Rev. 2:22).

I cut off the assignment of Jezebel against the ministers of God (1 Kings 19:2).

I cut off and break the powers of every word released by Jezebel against my life.

I cut off Jezebel's table and reject all food from it (1 Kings 18:19).

I cut off and loose myself from all curses of Jezebel and spirits of Jezebel operating in my bloodline.

I cut off the assignment of Jezebel and her daughters to corrupt the church.

I rebuke and cut off the spirit of Athaliah that attempts to destroy the royal seed (2 Kings 11:1).

I come against the spirit of Herodias and cut off the assignment to kill the prophets (Mark 6:22–24).

I rebuke and cut off the spirit of whoredoms (Hos. 4:12).

I rebuke and cut off Jezebel and her witchcrafts in the name of Jesus (2 Kings 9:22).

I rebuke and cut off the harlot and mistress of witchcrafts and break her power over my life and family (Nah. 3:4).

I cut off witchcrafts out of the hands (Mic. 5:12).

I overcome Jezebel and receive power over the nations (Rev. 2:26).

DEALING WITH SPIRITS OF THE DESERT

I speak to every desert in my life or ministry in the name of Jesus.

I bind and cast out any desert spirit sent against my life.

I bind and cast out every spirit of the desert owl, the desert fox, the desert dragon, the desert hyena, and the desert vulture in the name of Jesus (Isa. 34:11–15).

I bind and cast out every scorpion spirit of fear and torment in the name of Jesus (Deut. 8:15).

I bind and rebuke the screech owl in the name of Jesus (Isa. 34:14).

I bind and cast out every jackal in the name of Jesus (Ezek. 13:15).

I will not dwell in the wilderness but in a fruitful land (Isa. 35:1).

My desert shall blossom as a rose and bring forth abundant fruit (Isa. 35:1).

Release water in my dry places and streams in the desert (Isa. 35:6).

Let rivers flow into my desert places (Isa. 43:20).

I rebuke the beasts of the desert, every doleful creature, every satyr, and every dragon from operating in my life (Isa. 13:21–22).

Let your voice shake every wilderness place in my life (Ps. 29:8).

Let fatness drop upon my wilderness places (Ps. 65:11–12).

Let the spirits of the wilderness bow and lick the dust (Ps. 72:9).

I rebuke every pelican and owl of the wilderness (Ps. 102:6).

Turn the wilderness into a pool of water and the dry ground into water springs (Ps. 107:35).

Open rivers in high places, and fountains in the midst of the valleys, and make my wilderness places a pool of water and my dry places springs of water (Isa. 41:18).

Plant in my wilderness places the cedar, the shittah tree, the myrtle tree, the oil tree, the fir tree, the pine tree, and the box tree together (Isa. 41:19).

I renounce all rebellion that would open my life to desert spirits (Ps. 68:6).

I break every curse of trusting in man that would open my life to desert spirits (Jer. 17:5–6).

I prophesy to every dry bone in my life and command it to live (Ezek. 37:1–4).

My land shall not be termed desolate, but I am called Hephzi-bah, and my land Beulah (Isa. 62:4).

Make all my wilderness places like Eden, and my desert places like the garden of the Lord (Ps. 51:3).

Let every desolation in my life or bloodline be raised up in the name of Jesus (Isa. 61:4).

Revive me, and repair every desolation in my life (Ezra 9:9).

PRAYERS AGAINST DEMONIC HORSEMEN

Let the horse and rider be thrown into the sea (Exod. 15:1).

Break in pieces the horse and his rider. Break in pieces the chariot and his rider (Jer. 51:21).

I release the sword of the Lord upon the horses and chariots (Jer. 50:37).

I cut off the horses and destroy the chariots in the name of Jesus (Mic. 5:10).

Overthrow the chariots and those that ride them. Bring down the horses and their riders (Hag. 2:22).

Confound the riders on horses (Zech. 10:5).

Let the horses' heels be bitten, and let the riders fall backward (Gen. 49:17).

Let the chariot, the horse, the army, and the power lie down together and not be able to rise (Isa. 43:17).

Let the chariot and the horse be cast into a deep sleep at Your rebuke, O Lord (Ps. 76:6).

Make the horses afraid as the grasshopper (Job 39:19–20).

Let the chariots and horsemen be burned with Your fire (Nah. 2:13).

Smite the horses with astonishment and the riders with madness and blindness, O Lord (Zech. 12:4).

I bind and rebuke every black horse that would come against me in the name of Jesus (Rev. 6:5).

I bind and rebuke every red horse that would come against me in the name of Jesus (Rev. 6:4).

I bind and rebuke every pale horse that would come against me in the name of Jesus (Rev. 6:8).

Take away the strength of the demonic horsemen in the name of Jesus (Job 39:19).

Let the horses be cut by Your power, O Lord (2 Sam. 8:4).

I am Your goodly horse in the day of battle (Zech. 10:3).

Prayers Against Spirits of the Valley

I bind and cast out all spirits that would attempt to keep me in a low place in the name of Jesus.

I break the chariots of the enemies of the valley in the name of Jesus (Judg. 1:19).

I rebuke and cast out the ravens of the valley in the name of Jesus (Prov. 30:17).

Lord, You are the God of the valleys. Cast out every valley spirit in the name of Jesus (1 Kings 20:28).

Let me be exalted and the spirits of the valley be smitten by Your power (2 Sam. 8:13).

I bind and rebuke every Goliath that would challenge me in the valley (1 Sam. 17:1–4).

Let all the giants of the valley be destroyed (Josh. 15:8).

Fight against the spirits of the valley, and let my enemies be avenged in the valley (Josh. 10:12–14).

Let every Achan in my life be destroyed in the valley (Josh. 7:24–26).

I loose myself from every Delilah spirit operating in the valley (Judg. 16:4).

Let all my valley places be blessed in the name of Jesus (2 Chron. 20:26).

Open a door of hope in all my valleys (Hos. 2:15).

I destroy every Edomite spirit in the valley in the name of Jesus (2 Kings 14:7).

Let water flow into every valley place of my life (Joel 3:18).

Let every valley place in my life be exalted (Luke 3:5).

I smite Amalek and destroy him in the valley (1 Sam. 15:3–5).

I smite all the Midianites in the valley (Judg. 6:33–34).

DEALING WITH SPIRIT BIRDS

I bind and rebuke any unclean and hateful bird sent against my life by the enemy in the name of Jesus (Rev. 18:2).

I exercise my dominion over the unclean fowl of the air in the name of Jesus (Ps. 8:8).

Let every spirit bird sent against me be taken in the snare (Eccles. 9:12).

I bind and rebuke every spiritual vulture in the name of Jesus (Isa. 34:15).

I bind the operation of the screech owl (night monster) from operating against me in the name of Jesus (Isa. 34:14).

I bind and rebuke the cormorant (the vomiting pelican) from operating against my life in the name of Jesus (Isa. 34:11).

I bind and rebuke the bittern from operating against my life in the name of Jesus (Isa. 34:11).

I bind and rebuke any raven sent against my life in the name of Jesus (Isa. 34:11).

I bind and rebuke any demonic eagle and hawk sent against my life, and I command their nests to be destroyed in the name of Jesus (Job 39:26–30).

I pray these unclean birds would be caged in the name of Jesus (Jer. 5:27).

I bind and rebuke any unclean bird that would attempt to nest in my life in the name of Jesus.

Let every wandering bird be cast out of its nest in the name of Jesus (Isa. 16:2).

Let Your presence drive every unclean bird
away from my life (Jer. 4:25–26).

Let every fowl of heaven operating against my life
be consumed in the name of Jesus (Zeph. 1:3).

Let these birds flee and fly away at Your rebuke (Jer. 9:10).

Let me walk in the path of wisdom that
no fowl knows (Job 28:7, 21).

I will not be afraid of the terror by night, and I rebuke every
night bird that would attempt to visit me at night (Ps. 91:5).

I am not a companion to owls (Job 30:29).

Deliverance From Lions

I rebuke every lion that would stoop and couch down
to attack me in the name of Jesus (Gen. 49:9).

Through the strength of God, I break the jaws of the lion
and pluck the spoil out of his mouth (Judg. 14:5).

Deliver me from the paw of the lion (1 Sam. 17:37).

I rebuke the fierce lion that would hunt me (Job 10:16).

Don't let the lion tear my soul (Ps. 7:2).

I rebuke and expose any lion that would
wait secretly to catch me (Ps. 10:9).

I rebuke any lurking lions in the name of Jesus (Ps. 17:12).

I tread upon the lion in the name of Jesus (Ps. 91:3).

I walk in holiness, and no lion can dwell in my life (Isa. 35:9).

Deliver me from men who are like lions (1 Chron. 11:22).

Let the lion's whelps be scattered (Job 4:11).

Save me from the lion's mouth (Ps. 22:21).

Break the teeth of the lions (Ps. 58:6).

Deliver my soul from lions (Ps. 57:4).

Deliver me from the power of the lions (Dan. 6:7).

Deliver me out of the mouth of the lion (2 Tim. 4:17).

Let the Lion of the tribe of Judah roar
through me against my enemies.

Deliver me from the power of the lion.

DELIVERANCE FROM SERPENTS

Lord, bruise the head of every serpent that would
attack my life in the name of Jesus.

Punish the piercing serpent in the name of Jesus.

I bind and rebuke any serpent that would
try to deceive me (2 Cor. 11:3).

I release the rod of God to swallow up every serpent that
would come against me in the name of Jesus (Exod. 7:12).

Protect me from fiery serpents (Deut. 8:15).

I bind and rebuke every serpent that would try to
twist or coil around my life in the name of Jesus.

I bind and rebuke every python that would try to
squeeze out my prayer life in the name of Jesus.

I bind and rebuke every cobra that would
come against me in the name of Jesus.

I bind and rebuke every cockatrice that would come
against me in the name of Jesus (Isa. 14:29).

I bind and rebuke every flying serpent that would
attack my life in the name of Jesus (Isa. 27:1).

I bind and rebuke every sea serpent that would
attack my life in the name of Jesus (Isa. 27:1).

I have authority to tread upon serpents (Luke 10:19).

I am a believer, and I pick up serpents (Mark 16:18).

Let the fire of God drive out every serpent from my life (Acts 28:3).

I cast out every viper that would operate
in my life in the name of Jesus.

Deliverance From Flies

I bind and rebuke Beelzebub, the lord of the
flies, in the name of Jesus (Matt. 12:24).

I bind and cast out all flies that would attempt to affect
my anointing in the name of Jesus (Eccles. 10:1).

I bind and rebuke any swarm of flies that would come
against me in the name of Jesus (Ps. 78:45).

No flies can live in my life in the name of Jesus (Exod. 8:21).

I renounce and loose myself from any spiritual garbage
that would attract flies in the name of Jesus.

I rebuke every fly and every bee that would come
upon my land in the name of Jesus (Isa. 7:18).

Deliverance From Animalistic Spirits

I am delivered from the wild beasts of the desert (Isa. 34:14).

I rebuke the jackals that would attack my life,
city, or nation in the name of Jesus.

I rebuke the night wolves that would attack my life,
city, or nation in the name of Jesus (Hab. 1:8).

I rebuke every goat spirit of Pan, Faun,
and Satyr in the name of Jesus.

I rebuke the wild cats—leopards, lions, jaguars, which
represent higher occult powers—that would attack
my life, city, or nation in the name of Jesus.

I rebuke the hyenas that would attack my life, city, or nation in the name of Jesus (Isa. 34:14).

I rebuke and bind every wild dog (represents false religion, witchcraft, and perversion) that would hound my life in the name of Jesus (Ps. 22:16).

I bind and rebuke the bulls (represents strong rebellion) in the name of Jesus (Ps. 22:12).

I command all foxes that would destroy my fruit to leave my life in the name of Jesus.

SECTION 5

EXPERIENCING DELIVERANCE and RELEASE

ISRAEL EXPERIENCED MANY DELIVERANCES IN ITS HISTORY. The nation of Israel began with a mighty deliverance. David the king received many deliverances. He called upon the Lord for deliverance and was heard (Ps. 34:4). God answers the cries and prayers of His people. God's deliverance is always a sign of His love and mercy. The word *salvation* means deliverance. The Bible is filled with stories of deliverance and salvation.

One of the greatest revelations is the revelation of self-deliverance. We can loose ourselves from any control in darkness (Isa. 52:2). We can exercise power and authority for our own lives. Jesus told us to cast out the beam from our own eye (Luke 6:42). The term *cast out* is the same word used in reference to casting out demons (*ekballo*).

Take spiritual responsibility for your life. Don't depend on everyone else for your spiritual well-being. Confess the Word over your life. Pray strong prayers that rout the enemy. Do not allow self-pity to hold you back. Stir yourself up to prayer. This is a key to an overcoming life.

Those who experienced deliverance either came or were brought to Jesus. Someone had to take the initiative. It all begins with a decision. You cannot allow passivity to rob you of deliverance. You must open your mouth. Your deliverance is as close as your mouth.

There are many people frustrated with life. People who struggle can become overwhelmed by doubt and failure. Some are battling stress and pressure that often lead to emotional and physical problems. Jesus spent a considerable amount of time ministering to the oppressed. Multitudes came to hear Him in order to be healed and delivered from evil spirits.

Deliverance is the children's bread. Every child of God has a right to enjoy the benefits of deliverance. Deliverance brings freedom and joy. We have seen thousands of believers set free from demons through authoritative prayer. Deliverance is a miracle ministry. You will see multiplied miracles through warfare prayer.

The breakthroughs you will see are supernatural. Healings will multiply. Long-term bondages will be destroyed. Hidden roots will be exposed and eliminated. Inexplicable problems will be solved. Stubborn obstacles will be removed. Cycles of failure will be broken.

Frustration and despair will be eliminated through warfare prayer. Discouragement and disappointment will be overcome. The puzzling problems of life will be taken away. Lasting peace can finally be experienced. The abundant life can be enjoyed.

Failures that cause bitterness are reversed through warfare prayer. Prosperity and success will come. Advancement will be seen in different areas of your life. You will experience success in relationships, finances, ministry, and projects. Deliverance is designed to eliminate the spiritual obstacles that impede progress. Deliverance makes the rough places smooth and the crooked places straight.

You can see the enemy routed from your life. You can live free from the bondages and oppressions of demons. You can experience victory through prayer. Your words and prayers have tremendous power to destroy the works of darkness.

Those who experience deliverance and release will see notable changes. Sometimes the change is progressive and sometimes instantaneous. The change, however, will be dramatic. There will be an increase of joy, liberty, peace, and success. This will result in a better spiritual life with an increase of strength and holiness.

Patience is necessary to see breakthrough. God promised Israel that He would drive the enemy out little by little (Deut. 7:22; Exod. 23:29–30). Unless you understand this principle, you will become weary in praying for some people, and you will become discouraged in your own deliverance. The more freedom you will receive, the more you need to grow and possess your land.

You have the authority to bind and loose (Matt. 18:18). Webster's dictionary defines the word *bind* as, "to make secure by tying; to confine, restrain, or restrict *as* if with bonds: to constrain with legal authority: to exert a restraining or compelling effect." It also means to arrest, apprehend, handcuff, lead captive, take charge of, lock up, restrain, check, or put a stop to. Binding is done by legal authority. We have legal authority in the name of Jesus to bind the works of darkness.

The works of darkness encompass sin, iniquity, perversion, sickness, disease, infirmity, death, destruction, curses, witchcraft, sorcery, divination, poverty, lack, strife, lust, pride, rebellion, fear, torment, and confusion. We have legal authority to put a stop to these things in our lives and in the lives of those we minister to.

Loose means to untie, to free from restraint, to detach, to disjoin, divorce, separate, unhitch, get free, get loose, escape, break away, unbind, unchain, unfetter, free, release, unlock, liberate, disconnect, or forgive.

People need to be loosed from curses, evil inheritance,

familiar spirits, sin, guilt, shame, condemnation, control, domination, manipulation, intimidation, mind control, religious control, sickness, disease, deception, false teaching, sin, habits, worldliness, carnality, demons, tradition, ungodly soul ties, ungodly pledges, ungodly vows, spoken words, hexes, vexes, jinxes, trauma, and cults. We have legal authority in the name of Jesus to loose ourselves and others to whom we minister from these destroying influences.

Prayers for Self-Deliverance

I break all generational curses of pride, rebellion, lust, poverty, witchcraft, idolatry, death, destruction, failure, sickness, infirmity, fear, schizophrenia, and rejection in the name of Jesus.

I command all generational and hereditary spirits operating in my life through curses to be bound and cast out in the name of Jesus.

I command all spirits of lust, perversion, adultery, fornication, uncleanness, and immorality to come out of my sexual character in the name of Jesus.

I command all spirits of hurt, rejection, fear, anger, wrath, sadness, depression, discouragement, grief, bitterness, and unforgiveness to come out of my emotions in the name of Jesus.

I command all spirits of confusion, forgetfulness, mind control, mental illness, doublemindedness, fantasy, pain, pride, and memory recall to come out of my mind in the name of Jesus.

I break all curses of schizophrenia and command all spirits of doublemindedness, rejection, rebellion, and root of bitterness to come out in the name of Jesus.

I command all spirits of guilt, shame, and condemnation to come out of my conscience in the name of Jesus.

I command all spirits of pride, stubbornness, disobedience, rebellion, self-will, selfishness, and arrogance to come out of my will in the name of Jesus.

I command all spirits of addiction to come out of my appetite in the name of Jesus.

I command all spirits of witchcraft, sorcery, divination, and occult to come out in the name of Jesus.

I command all spirits operating in my head, eyes, mouth, tongue, and throat to come out in the name of Jesus.

I command all spirits operating in my chest and lungs to come out in the name of Jesus.

I command all spirits operating in my back and spine to come out in the name of Jesus.

I command all spirits operating in my stomach, navel, and abdomen to come out in the name of Jesus.

I command all spirits operating in my heart, spleen, kidneys, liver, and pancreas to come out in the name of Jesus.

I command all spirits operating in my sexual organs to come out in the name of Jesus.

I command all spirits operating in my hands, arms, legs, and feet to come out in the name of Jesus.

I command all demons operating in my skeletal system, including my bones, joints, knees, and elbows, to come out in the name of Jesus.

I command all spirits operating in my glands and endocrine system to come out in the name of Jesus.

I command all spirits operating in my blood and circulatory systems to come out in the name of Jesus.

I command all spirits operating in my muscles and muscular system to come out in the name of Jesus.

I command all religious spirits of doubt, unbelief, error, heresy, and tradition that came in through religion to come out in the name of Jesus.

I command all spirits from my past that are hindering my present and future to come out in the name of Jesus.

I command all ancestral spirits that entered through my ancestors to come out in the name of Jesus.

I command all hidden spirits hiding in any part of my life to come out in the name of Jesus.

Prayers for Prosperity and Financial Release

I break all assignments of the enemy against my finances in the name of Jesus.

I break all curses of poverty, lack, debt, and failure in the name of Jesus.

I seek first the kingdom of God and His righteousness, and all things are added unto me (Matt. 6:33).

I rebuke and cast out all spirits of the cankerworm, palmerworm, caterpillar, and locust that would eat up my blessings in the name of Jesus (Joel 2:25).

Lord, teach me to profit, and lead me in the way I should go (Isa. 48:17).

You are Jehovah-Jireh, my provider (Gen. 22:14).

You are El Shaddai, the God of more than enough.

Wealth and riches are in my house because I fear You and delight greatly in Your commandments (Ps. 112:1–3).

The blessing of the Lord upon my life makes me rich.

I am blessed coming in and blessed going out.

I am God's servant, and He takes pleasure in my prosperity (Ps. 35:27).

Jesus, You became poor, that through Your poverty I might be rich (2 Cor. 8:9).

I meditate on the Word day and night, and whatever I do prospers (Ps. 1:3).

Let peace be within my walls and prosperity within my palace (Ps. 122:7).

I will prosper through the prophets and prophetic ministry (Ezra 6:14).

I believe the prophets, and I prosper (2 Chron. 20:20).

I am Your servant, Lord. Prosper me (Neh. 1:11).

The God of heaven will prosper me (Neh. 2:20).

I live in the prosperity of the King (Jer. 23:5).

Through Your favor I will be a prosperous person (Gen. 39:2).

Lord, You have called me, and You will make
my way prosperous (Isa. 48:15).

I pray in secret, and You reward me openly (Matt. 6:6).

I fast in secret, and You reward me openly (Matt. 6:18).

You reward me because I diligently seek You (Heb. 11:6).

Lord, release the wealth of the wicked into my hands (Prov. 13:22).

Lord, bring me into a wealthy place (Ps. 66:12).

I give, and it is given to me—good measure, pressed
down, shaken together, and running over (Luke 6:38).

Open the floodgates of heaven over my life, and I receive
more than I have enough room to receive (Mal. 3:10).

Let every hole in my bag be closed in
the name of Jesus (Hag. 1:6).

Rebuke the devourer for my sake (Mal. 3:11).

All nations will call me blessed, and I will
be a delightful land (Mal. 3:12).

My gates are open continually that the forces (wealth)
of the nations can come into my life (Isa. 60:11).

I am in league with the stones of the field (Job 5:23).

Let Your showers of blessing come upon my life (Ezek. 34:26).

Let my vats overflow (Joel 2:24).

Let my barns be filled with plenty and my
presses burst with new wine (Prov. 3:10).

Command Your blessing upon my storehouse (Deut. 28:8).

Let my barns be full and overflowing. Let my sheep bring forth thousands and ten thousands. Let my oxen be strong to labor (Ps. 144:13–14).

The plowman overtakes the reaper in my life, and the treader of grapes the sower of the seed, and I live in continual harvest (Amos 9:13).

Let my floor be full of wheat and my vats overflow with wine and oil (Joel 2:24).

Deal wondrously with me, and let me eat and be satisfied (Joel 2:26).

Make peace within my border, and fill me with the finest of wheat (Ps. 147:14).

Let me be filled with honey and the finest of wheat (Ps. 81:16).

Lead me into the land flowing with milk and honey (Exod. 3:8).

Bring me into a good land without scarceness and lack (Deut. 8:9).

Make all grace abound toward me that I will have sufficiency in all things and abound to every good work (2 Cor. 9:8).

Anoint my head with oil, and let my cup run over (Ps. 23:5).

Let me have riches and honor in abundance (2 Chron. 18:1).

Let the rock pour me out rivers of oil (Job 29:6).

Let me dip my feet in oil (Deut. 33:24).

Let me see Your heaps in my life (2 Chron. 31:8).

I love wisdom, I inherit substance, and my treasures are filled (Prov. 8:21).

I receive riches and honor, durable riches and righteousness (Prov. 8:18).

Bring honey out of the rock for me (Ps. 81:16).

Let me eat the finest of wheat (Ps. 147:14).

Let my teeth be white with milk (Gen. 49:12).

Wash my steps with butter (Job 29:6).

Let me lay up gold as dust (Job 22:24).

Let me have plenty of silver (Job 28:1).

Let Your river lead me to gold (Gen. 2:11–12).

Let me inherit the land (Ps. 37:29).

I refuse to allow the angel of blessing to depart without blessing me (Gen. 2:6).

Prayers for Healing and Health

I am healed by the stripes of Jesus (Isa. 53:5).

Jesus carried my sickness and infirmities (Matt. 8:17).

I cast out all spirits of infirmity that would attack my body in the name of Jesus.

I break, rebuke, and cast out any spirit of cancer that would attempt to establish itself in my lungs, bones, breast, throat, back, spine, liver, kidneys, pancreas, skin, or stomach in the name of Jesus.

I rebuke and cast out all spirits causing diabetes, high blood pressure, low blood pressure, heart attack, stroke, kidney failure, leukemia, blood disease, breathing problems, arthritis, lupus, Alzheimer's, or insomnia in the name of Jesus.

I speak healing and strength to my bones, muscles, joints, organs, head, eyes, throat, glands, blood, marrow, lungs, kidneys, liver, spleen, spine, pancreas, eyes, bladder, ears, nose, sinuses, mouth, tongue, and feet in the name of Jesus.

I loose myself from all heart attacks rooted in fear, and I command all spirits of fear to leave in Jesus's name (Luke 21:26).

I loose myself from all diabetes rooted in rejection, self-hatred, inheritance, and guilt, and I command these spirits to come out in the name of Jesus.

I loose myself from all cancer rooted in bitterness, unforgiveness, resentment, and slander of the tongue, and I command these spirits to come out in the name of Jesus.

I loose myself from lupus rooted in self-rejection, self-hatred, and guilt, and I cast these spirits out in the name of Jesus.

I loose myself from all multiple sclerosis rooted in self-hatred, guilt, and rejection from the father, and I cast these spirits out in the name of Jesus.

I loose myself from rheumatoid arthritis that is rooted in self-hatred and low self-esteem, and I command these spirits to come out in the name of Jesus.

I loose myself from high cholesterol that is rooted in anger and hostility and command these spirits to come out in the name of Jesus.

I loose myself from all sinus problems rooted in fear and anxiety, and I command these spirits to come out in the name of Jesus.

I loose myself from all high blood pressure rooted in fear and anxiety, and I command these spirits to come out in the name of Jesus.

I loose myself from asthma rooted in fear concerning relationships in the name of Jesus.

I loose myself from a weakened immune system that is rooted in a broken spirit or broken heart, and I command these spirits to come out in the name of Jesus.

I loose myself from all strokes rooted in self-rejection, self-bitterness, and self-hatred, and I command these spirits to come out in the name of Jesus.

I loose myself from all bone diseases rooted in
envy and jealousy, and I command these spirits to
come out in the name of Jesus (Prov. 14:30).

Forgive me, Lord, for allowing any fear, guilt, self-
rejection, self-hatred, unforgiveness, bitterness, sin,
pride, or rebellion to open the door to any sickness or
infirmity. I renounce these things in the name of Jesus.

I cast out any spirit of infirmity that came into
my life through pride in the name of Jesus.

I cast out any spirit of infirmity that came into my life
through trauma or accidents in the name of Jesus.

I cast out any spirit of infirmity that came into my
life through rejection in the name of Jesus.

I cast out any spirit of infirmity that came into my
life through witchcraft in the name of Jesus.

Give me a sound heart, which is the life of my flesh.
Remove from my heart any evil or sinful attitude.

Lord, remove any darts from my liver (Prov. 7:23).

Heal and deliver me from all my pains in the name of Jesus.

I rebuke any sickness that would come to eat up my flesh,
including cancer, in the name of Jesus (Ps. 27:2).

Let no evil diseases (things of Belial) cleave to my body (Ps. 41:8).

I break all curses of sickness and disease, and I command
all hereditary spirits of sickness to come out (Gal. 3:13).

I break all curses of premature death and
destruction in the name of Jesus.

I prosper and walk in health even as my soul prospers (3 John 2).

I receive the Word of God, which is health to my flesh (Prov. 4:22).

Lord, bless my bread and water, and take
sickness away from me (Exod. 23:25).

I command every organ in my body to function
the way God intended (Ps. 139:14).

My bones are fat because I receive the good
report of the gospel (Prov. 15:30).

Lord, keep all my bones (Ps. 34:20).

Let every tumor or evil growth melt at
the presence of God (Ps. 97:5).

Let any infection in my body be burned by the fire of God.

I release myself from all allergies and sinus
problems in the name of Jesus.

I pray for my arteries and blood vessels to be opened and my
circulatory system to function properly in the name of Jesus.

I rebuke all fevers in the name of Jesus (Luke 4:39).

My flesh shall be fresher than a child's, and I will
return to the days of my youth (Job 33:25).

I pray for my immune system to be strengthened
in the name of Jesus (Ps. 119:28).

Lord, renew my youth like the eagle's (Ps. 103:5).

I will live and not die, and I will proclaim
the name of the Lord (Ps. 118:17).

My beauty shall be as the olive tree (Hos. 14:6).

Lord, You heal all of my diseases (Ps. 103:3).

Lord, You are the health of my countenance (Ps. 43:5).

Heal me, O Lord, and I shall be healed (Jer. 17:14).

Let Your virtue touch my life and heal me (Luke 6:19).

I release the fire of God to burn out any sickness or disease
that would operate in my body in the name of Jesus.

No sickness or plague will come near my dwelling (Ps. 91:10).

Jesus, arise over my life with healing in Your wings (Mal. 4:2).

The Lord is the strength of my life (Ps. 27:1).

I command every germ or sickness that touches
my body to die in the name of Jesus.

I take the shield of faith and quench every
fiery dart of the enemy (Eph. 6:16).

I am redeemed from sickness and disease (Gal. 3:13).

Every plague is stopped when it comes near me through
the atonement of Jesus Christ (Num. 16:50).

I loose myself from every infirmity (Luke 13:12).

Jesus Christ makes me whole (Acts 9:34).

I am fearfully and wonderfully made. Let my body function in
the wonderful way You designed it to function (Ps. 139:14).

Prayers of Deliverance

Keep my soul, and deliver me (Ps. 25:20).

Be pleased, O Lord, to deliver me (Ps. 40:13).

Make haste, O God, and deliver me (Ps. 70:1).

Deliver me in Your righteousness (Ps. 71:2).

Deliver me, O God, out of the hand of the enemy (Ps. 71:4).

Deliver me from my persecutors (Ps. 142:6).

Deliver me out of great waters (Ps. 144:7).

Deliver me from the oppression of man (Ps. 119:134).

Deliver me according to Your Word (Ps. 119:170).

Deliver my soul from lying lips and a deceitful tongue (Ps. 120:2).

Deliver me from my enemies, and hide me (Ps. 143:9).

Surround me with songs of deliverance (Ps. 32:7).

Command deliverances for my life (Ps. 44:4).

Deliver me from all my fears (Ps. 34:4).

Deliver me out of all my trouble (Ps. 54:7).

Deliver me from them who hate me (Ps. 69:14).

Deliver me out of my distresses (Ps. 107:6).

Send Your Word, and deliver me out of destruction (Ps. 107:20).

Deliver my soul from death, my eyes from tears, and my feet from falling (Ps. 116:8).

I call upon the name of Jesus, and I am delivered (Joel 2:32).

Deliver me from the power of the lion (Dan. 6:27).

Through Your knowledge I am delivered (Prov. 11:9).

Through Your wisdom I am delivered (Prov. 28:26).

I receive miracles of deliverance for my life (Dan. 6:27).

Prayers for Deliverance From Evil

Deliver me from evil (Matt. 6:13).

I pray that You would keep me from evil (1 Chron. 4:10).

No evil will touch me (Job 5:19).

Put to shame those who wish me evil (Ps. 40:14).

Let no evil disease cleave to my body (Ps. 41:8).

I will not be afraid of evil tidings (Ps. 112:7).

I will not be visited with evil (Prov. 19:23).

I refrain my feet from every evil way so that I might keep Your Word (Ps. 119:101).

Preserve me from all evil (Ps. 121:7).

Deliver me from the evil man (Ps. 140:1).

Let people be healed of plagues and evil spirits (Luke 7:21).

I pray that You would keep me from evil (John 17:15).

Let evil spirits be cast out (Acts 19:12).

I will not be overcome with evil, but I overcome evil with good (Rom. 12:21).

I put on the whole armor of God that I might stand in the evil day (Eph. 6:13).

I cancel all the plans and forces of evil sent against my life.

Let the works of evil be burned by Your holy fire.

Let men repent of evil and turn to righteousness.

Let no evil be established in my life, but let Your righteousness be established.

I loose myself from all evildoers and evil soul ties.

DELIVERANCE AND RENUNCIATION OF SEXUAL SIN

I renounce all sexual sin that I have been involved with in the past, including fornication, masturbation, pornography, perversion, fantasy, and adultery in the name of Jesus.

I break all curses of adultery, perversion, fornication, lust, incest, rape, molestation, illegitimacy, harlotry, and polygamy in the name of Jesus.

I command all spirits of lust and perversion to come out of my stomach, genitals, eyes, mind, mouth, hands, and blood in the name of Jesus.

I present my body to the Lord as a living sacrifice (Rom. 12:1).

My members are the members of Christ. I will not let them be the members of a harlot (1 Cor. 6:15).

I release the fire of God to burn out all unclean lust from my life in the name of Jesus.

I break all ungodly soul ties with former lovers and sexual partners in the name of Jesus.

I cast out all spirits of loneliness that would drive me to ungodly sexual relationships in the name of Jesus.

I command all spirits of hereditary lusts from my ancestors to come out in the name of Jesus.

I command all spirits of witchcraft that work with lust to leave in the name of Jesus.

I take authority over my thoughts and bind all spirits of fantasy and lustful thinking in the name of Jesus.

I cast out all marriage-breaking spirits of lust that would break covenant in the name of Jesus.

I cast out and loose myself from any spirit spouses and spirits of incubus and succubus in the name of Jesus.

I cast out all spirits of perversion, including Moabite and Ammonite spirits of lust, in the name of Jesus.

I receive the spirit of holiness in my life to walk in sexual purity in the name of Jesus (Rom. 1:4).

I loose myself from the spirit of the world, the lust of the flesh, the lust of the eyes, and the pride of life. I overcome the world through the power of the Holy Spirit (1 John 2:16).

I am crucified with Christ. I mortify my members. I do not let sin reign in my body, and I will not obey its lust (Rom. 6:6–12).

PRAYERS FOR ANGELIC DELIVERANCE

Let Your angels ascend and descend upon my life (Gen. 28:12).

Give Your angels charge over me, and deliver me (Ps. 91:11).

Let the angel of the Lord chase the enemy (Ps. 35:5).

Let the angel of the Lord persecute the enemy (Ps. 35:6).

Let Your angels fight for me in the heavens
against principalities (Dan. 10:13).

Let the angel of Your presence save me (Isa. 63:9).

Let Your angels go before me and make the
crooked places straight (Zech. 12:8).

Send Your angels before me to prosper my way (Exod. 33:2).

Lord, hear my voice and send Your angels to deliver me (Num. 20:16).

Send Your angels to minister unto me (Matt. 4:11).

I have come to Zion and to an innumerable
company of angels (Heb. 12:22).

I am an heir of salvation. Send Your angels
to minister to me (Heb. 1:14).

Send Your angels to deliver me from the
hand of the enemy (Matt. 12:11).

Lord, confess me before Your holy angels (Luke 12:8).

Send Your angels in the night to minister to me (Acts 27:23).

Let Your angels meet me as I walk in my destiny (Gen. 32:1).

Send Your angels to be involved in reaching the lost (Acts 8:26).

Release Your angelic army to fight for and
defend Your church (Ps. 68:17).

Send Your angels to smite the demons that
come to destroy me (Isa. 37:36).

PRAYERS AGAINST TERRORISM

I bind and rebuke every red eagle of terror that would come
against my nation in the name of Jesus (Jer. 49:22).

I will not be afraid of the terror by night (Ps. 91:5).

I bind and rebuke all terrorists that would plot
against my nation in the name of Jesus.

I bind and rebuke all spirits of hatred and murder that would manifest through terrorism in the name of Jesus.

I bind and rebuke all religious terrorists in the name of Jesus.

I bind and rebuke all demons of jihad in the name of Jesus.

I bind and rebuke all spirits of antichrist and hatred of Christianity in the name of Jesus.

I bind all spirits of hatred of America in the name of Jesus.

I bind and rebuke the terrors of death in the name of Jesus (Ps. 55:4).

I bind all fear and panic that would come through terrorism in the name of Jesus.

Deliver me from violent and bloodthirsty men (Ps. 140:1).

I cut the acts of violence out of the hands of the wicked (Isa. 59:6).

Let the assemblies of violent men be exposed and cut off (Ps. 86:14).

Let violence be no more in my borders (Isa. 60:18).

Apostolic Prayers

Father, keep me from all evil (John 17:15).

Sanctify me through Your Word of truth (John 17:17).

Let me be one with my brothers and sisters that the world might believe I have been sent (John 17:21).

My heart's desire and prayer for Israel is that they might be saved (Rom. 10:1).

Let me be counted worthy of my calling and fulfill all the good pleasure of Your goodness and the work of faith with power (2 Thess. 1:11).

Let Your Word have free course in my life (2 Thess. 3:1).

Give me the spirit of wisdom and revelation
in the knowledge of Jesus (Eph. 1:17).

Let the eyes of my understanding be enlightened that I might
know what is the hope of my calling, what are the riches of the
glory of Your inheritance in the saints, and what is the exceeding
greatness of Your power toward me who believes (Eph. 1:17–19).

Strengthen me with might by Your Spirit
in the inner man (Eph. 3:16).

Let Christ dwell in my heart by faith, and let me be
rooted and grounded in love, and let me comprehend
with all saints what is the breadth and length and
depth and height of Your love (Eph. 3:17–18).

Let me know the love of Christ, which passes all understanding,
that I might be filled with all the fullness of God (Eph. 3:19).

Lord, do exceeding abundantly above all I can ask or think,
according to the power that works in me (Eph. 3:20).

Let utterance be given unto me, that I may open my mouth
boldly to make known the mystery of the gospel (Eph. 6:19).

Let my love abound more and more in knowledge
and in all judgment (Phil. 1:9).

Let me approve things that are excellent, that I might be sincere
and without offense until the day of Christ (Phil. 1:10).

Let me know Jesus and the power of His resurrection
and the fellowship of His sufferings, being made
conformable unto His death (Phil. 3:10).

Let me be filled with the knowledge of Your will in all wisdom
and spiritual understanding, that I might walk worthy of
You unto all pleasing, being fruitful in every good work
and increasing in the knowledge of God (Col. 1:9–10).

Let me be strengthened with all might according to Your glorious power, unto all patience and longsuffering with joyfulness (Col. 1:11).

Let me stand perfect and complete in all the will of God (Col. 4:12).

Let my whole spirit and soul and body be preserved blameless unto the coming of my Lord Jesus Christ (1 Thess. 5:23).

Lord, give me peace always by all means, and be with me (2 Thess. 3:16).

I make supplication, intercession, and give thanks for all men and leaders in my nation and in the church, that I might lead a quiet and peaceable life in all godliness and honesty (1 Tim. 2:1–2).

I receive multiplied grace and peace through the apostolic anointing (2 Pet. 1:2).

BINDING AND LOOSING

I have the keys of the kingdom, and whatever I bind on Earth is bound in heaven, and whatever I loose on Earth is loosed in heaven (Matt. 16:19).

I bind the kings in chains and the nobles with fetters of iron (Ps. 149:8).

I bind the strongman and spoil his goods (Matt. 12:29).

I bind leviathan and all proud spirits arrayed against my life (Job 41:5).

I bind the principalities, powers, rulers of the darkness of this world, and spiritual wickedness in high places (Eph. 6:12).

I bind all sickness and disease released against my mind or body.

Let the exiles be loosed (Isa. 51:14).

Let the prisoners be loosed (Ps. 146:7).

Loose those appointed to death (Ps. 102:20).

I loose my neck from all bands (Isa. 52:2).

I loose myself from the bands of wickedness (Isa. 58:6).

I loose myself from the bands of Orion (Job 38:31).

I loose myself from all bonds (Ps. 116:16).

I loose my mind, will, and emotions from every assignment and spirit of darkness in the name of Jesus.

I loose my city and region from every assignment of hell.

I loose my finances from every spirit of poverty, debt, and lack.

I loose myself from all generational curses and hereditary spirits (Gal. 3:13).

I loose myself from every assignment of witchcraft, sorcery, and divination.

I loose myself from every spoken curse and negative word spoken against my life.

RELEASING SHAME UPON THE ENEMY

Let the enemy be ashamed and sore vexed. Let them return and be ashamed suddenly (Ps. 6:10).

Show me a token for good that they which hate me may see and be ashamed (Ps. 86:17).

Put to shame those who seek after my soul (Ps. 35:4).

Let those who seek to hurt me be clothed with shame (Ps. 35:26).

Scatter their bones, and put them to shame (Ps. 53:5).

Let those who seek after my soul be ashamed and confounded; let those who desire my hurt be turned backward and put to confusion (Ps. 70:2).

Fill their faces with shame (Ps. 83:16).

Let all those incensed against You be ashamed (Isa. 45:24).

Let those who arise against me be ashamed (Ps. 109:28).

Let the proud spirits be ashamed (Ps. 119:78).

Prayers for Souls

All souls belong to You, O Lord (Ezek. 18:4).

Lord, You are the shepherd and bishop of my soul.
Watch over my soul and keep it (1 Pet. 2:25).

I receive with meekness the engrafted word that
is able to save my soul (James 1:21).

I bind the hunter of souls (Ezek. 13:20).

In patience I possess my soul (Luke 21:19).

I bind and tear off every veil used to hunt
souls and make them fly (Ezek. 13:20).

I command the souls that are hunted by the
enemy to be let go (Ezek. 13:20).

I release the souls from divination and witchcraft (Ezek. 13:23).

Return, O Lord, and deliver my soul (Ps. 6:4).

Let not the enemy persecute my soul (Ps. 7:5).

Lord, restore my soul (Ps. 23:3).

Keep my soul, and deliver me (Ps. 25:20).

Put to shame those who seek after my soul (Ps. 35:4).

Rescue my soul from destruction (Ps. 35:17).

Let those who seek after my soul be ashamed
and confounded (Ps. 40:14).

Deliver me from all oppressors who seek after my soul (Ps. 54:3).

Lord, You have delivered my soul from death
and my feet from falling (Ps. 56:13).

Preserve my soul, for I am holy (Ps. 86:2).

Rejoice my soul, for I lift up my soul unto You (Ps. 86:4).

Lord, Your comforts delight my soul (Ps. 94:19).

I break the power of all negative words
spoken against my soul (Ps. 109:20).

Return unto your rest, O my soul (Ps. 116:7).

My soul shall live and praise the Lord (Ps. 119:175).

My soul is escaped as a bird out of the
snare of the fowler (Ps. 124:7).

Strengthen me with strength in my soul (Ps. 138:3).

Destroy all who afflict my soul (Ps. 143:12).

Let Your fear come upon every soul in my city (Acts 2:43).

I will prosper and be in health, even as my soul prospers (3 John 2).

I pray my soul will be preserved blameless unto
the coming of the Lord (1 Thess. 5:23).

Satiate my soul with fatness (Jer. 31:14).

My soul will be joyful in the Lord. You have covered me with the
garments of salvation and the robe of righteousness (Isa. 61:10).

I break all ungodly soul ties and pray for godly soul ties
that will bring blessing to my life (1 Sam. 18:1).

I loose my soul from any oaths, inner vows, and
curses that would bind it in the name of Jesus.

PRAYERS FOR YOUR NATION

I pray for the leaders of my nation to come to the light (Isa. 60:3).

I make supplication, prayer, intercession, and give
thanks for all the people of my nation and for the
leaders of my nation, that I might live a peaceable
life in all godliness and honesty (1 Tim. 2:1–2).

Let our leaders be just, and let them rule by
the fear of the Lord (2 Sam. 23:3).

Let our leaders fall down before the Lord, and
let my nation serve Him (Ps. 72:11).

Let the poor and needy people of my nation
be delivered (Ps. 72:12–13).

Let the Lord's dominion be established in my nation,
and let His enemies lick the dust (Ps. 72:8–9).

Turn our leaders' hearts to fear You (Prov. 21:1)

Let the Lord rule over my nation, and let my
nation be glad and rejoice (Ps. 97:1)

Let my nation sing a new song, bless His name, and show
forth His salvation from day to day (Ps. 96:1–3)

Let the people of my nation tremble at the
presence of the Lord (Ps. 99:1).

Let my nation make a joyful noise to the Lord, and let
the people serve Him with gladness (Ps. 110:1–2).

Let our leaders praise You, and let them hear
the words of Your mouth (Ps. 138:4).

Let the wicked be rooted out of our land (Prov. 2:22).

Let the wicked be cut down and wither
as the green herb (Ps. 37:2).

Let all the people of my nation turn to the
Lord and worship Him (Ps. 22:27).

My nation is the Lord's and the fullness thereof,
and all they that dwell therein (Ps. 24:1).

Let all the idolaters in my nation be confounded, and
let all the gods worship the Lord (Ps. 97:7).

Let my nation praise the Lord for His merciful
kindness and truth (Ps. 117).

Save my nation, O Lord, and send prosperity (Ps. 118:25).

I pray that my nation will submit to the rule
and reign of Christ (Dan. 7:14).

I pray my nation will bring its wealth
into the kingdom (Rev. 21:24).

I pray my nation will be converted and bring
its wealth to the king (Isa. 60:5).

I pray my nation will be healed by the leaves
from the tree of life (Rev. 22:2).

I pray my nation will show forth the praises of God (Isa. 60:6).

I pray my nation will see the glory of God (Isa. 35:2).

Let those who are deaf hear the words of the book,
and let the blind see out of obscurity (Isa. 29:18).

I pray that Jesus will rule over my nation in
righteousness and judgment (Isa. 32:1).

I pray my nation will come to Zion to be taught,
and learn war no more (Isa. 2:1–4).

I pray that my nation will seek the Lord
and enter into His rest (Isa. 11:1).

I pray that the parched places in my nation will become a
pool, and every thirsty part springs of water (Isa. 35:7).

I pray that the glory of the Lord be revealed to my nation,
and that all the inhabitants will see it (Isa. 40:5).

Let the Lord bring righteousness and
judgment to my nation (Isa. 42:1).

I ask the Lord to do a new thing in my nation by giving waters
in the wilderness and streams in the desert (Isa. 43:19–20).

Let peace (shalom) come into my nation like a river (Isa. 66:12).

Let my nation be sprinkled by the blood of Jesus (Isa. 52:12).

Let the children of my nation be taught of the Lord (Isa. 54:13).

I pray that my nation will seek and find the Lord (Isa. 65:1).

Let my nation be filled with priests and Levites
that worship the Lord (Isa. 66:21).

Let the people of my nation come and
worship the Lord (Isa. 66:23).

Let my people build houses and inhabit them (Isa. 65:21).

Let my people plant vineyards and eat
the fruit of them (Isa. 65:21).

Let my people long enjoy the work of their hands (Isa. 65:22).

Let the enemies in my land be reconciled (Isa. 65:25).

Let my nation be filled with the knowledge
of the glory of the Lord (Hab. 2:14).

Let my nation be saved and walk in the light of Zion (Rev. 21:24).

Let God be merciful unto us and bless us, and cause
His face to shine upon us. Let His way be known to us,
and His saving health in our nation (Ps. 67:1–2).

Let every covenant with death and hell be
broken in our nation (Isa. 28:18).

Let my nation look to the Lord and be saved (Isa. 45:22).

Let the Lord make bare His holy arm, and let my
nation see the salvation of the Lord (Isa. 52:10).

Let every veil spread over my nation be destroyed (Isa. 25:7).

My nation is the inheritance of the Lord;
let Him possess it (Ps. 2:7–8).

The kingdom is the Lord's, and He is the
governor of my nation (Ps. 22:28).

Let the people who walk in darkness in my nation
see the light, and let Your light shine upon those
in the shadow of darkness (Isa. 9:2).

Let His government and peace (shalom)
continually increase in my nation (Isa. 9:7).

Let His justice and judgment increase in my nation (Isa. 9:7).

Let those in my nation who were not Your people be
called the children of the living God (Rom. 9:25–26).

Let righteousness, peace, and joy in the Holy
Ghost increase in my nation (Rom. 14:17).

I pray for righteousness to come to my nation, and
that my nation would be exalted (Prov. 14:34).

Let His Spirit be poured out in my nation, and let our
sons and daughters prophesy (Acts 2:17–18).

I will confess You, Lord, among my people
and sing unto Your name (Ps. 22:22).

Let Your glory be declared among my people, and
Your wonders in my nation (Ps. 96:20).

Open a door of utterance in my nation, that my
people might hear Your Word (Col. 4:3).

I pray that the families of my people be blessed
through Christ (Gen. 28:14, Gal. 3:14).

I pray for the healing waters to flow into my nation (Ezek. 47:9).